The Ballad of
BILLY AND GEORGE

The Ballad of
BILLY AND GEORGE

The Tempestuous Baseball Marriage of Billy Martin and George Steinbrenner

Phil Pepe

LYONS PRESS
Guilford, Connecticut
An imprint of Globe Pequot Press

Copyright © 2008 by Phil Pepe
First Lyons Press paperback edition 2010

Lyons Press is an imprint of Globe Pequot Press.

Photo on page i by Dan Farrell/*New York Daily News*

Text design by Sheryl P. Kober

The Library of Congress cataloged the hardcover edition as follows:

Pepe, Phil.
    The ballad of Billy and George : the tempestuous baseball marriage of Billy Martin
and George Steinbrenner / by Phil Pepe.
        p. cm.
    Includes bibliographical references and index.
    ISBN 978-1-59921-282-1
    1. Martin, Billy, 1928-1989. 2. Baseball managers—United States—Biography.
3. Steinbrenner, George M. (George Michael), 1930- 4. Baseball team owners—
United States—Biography. 5. New York Yankees (Baseball team) I. Title.
    GV865.A1P415 2008
    796.3570922—dc22
    [B]

                                                                        2008003573

ISBN 978-0-7627-7066-3

Printed in the United States of America
10 9 8 7 6 5 4 3 2 1

Contents

Preface

It was the best of times, it was the worst of times to be a baseball writer in New York City.

I was assigned by the *New York Daily News* to cover the Yankees in 1970 BS (before Steinbrenner) in the midst of the team's longest drought since they won their first American League pennant in 1921. The Yankees would go 11 long years without reaching the World Series, finishing higher than fourth place just three times in that span.

And then came the resurgence. It began in 1973, when a group led by George M. Steinbrenner, a shipbuilder from Cleveland and Lorain, Ohio, purchased the team from the Columbia Broadcasting System.

Two years later, Billy Martin came aboard, hired to manage the team for which he had excelled in World Series past, and ushered in the most turbulent era in Yankee history. The best of times, the worst of times.

Following a pattern he had established in Minnesota, Detroit, and Texas, Martin would make an immediate positive impact on the Yankees and end their pennantless drought in 1976, his first full season as manager. The following year, fortified by the arrival of slugger Reggie Jackson and overcoming unspeakable obstacles of controversy, turmoil, and discord, Martin and Jackson would put aside their differences and their open hostility toward one another and lead the Yankees to their first World Series championship in 15 years.

Together, Steinbrenner and Martin would return the Yankees to the glory years of the team's illustrious past. Theirs was a tempestuous love-hate relationship, not unlike ill-starred lovers who battled repeatedly, who needed one another. They parted frequently and reconciled just as frequently. Five times Martin was hired by Steinbrenner to manage the team, and five times Martin was fired as manager.

The best of times were the games, between the lines. Reggie Jackson's three home runs in Game 6 of the 1977 World Series. The remarkable comeback from a 14-game deficit in 1978. Bucky Dent's home run in the playoff game in Boston. Ron Guidry's 18 strikeouts against the California Angels.

The worst of times were after the games, in the clubhouse, in bars, and in the many dismissals of Martin as Yankees manager, the first in 1978.

Covering a team owned by the manipulative, meddlesome Steinbrenner, directed by the fiery, combative Martin, and manned by such divergent, disparate, and often contentious personalities as Jackson, Thurman Munson, Mickey Rivers, and Lou Piniella was as close as a chronicler of fun and games can get to being on the front lines as a war correspondent.

On the road, those of us who were beat writers were reluctant to sleep for fear that while we slumbered, one Yankee or another—in all likelihood the manager—would be involved in a barroom brawl. We were there, but we couldn't be everywhere, and we opened the next day's rival newspapers with trepidation that we had been scooped, angry if we were, grateful for another day's peace if we weren't.

Looking back three decades later, it's mind-boggling to think of all that was crammed into such a short period of time, the daily grind, the good and the bad, the highs and the lows. Had we known what this job entailed, to a man we might not have wanted it. But having done it, we're glad we persevered.

In assembling material for this book, I drew on a multitude of sources, countless interviews over a 13-year period with the principals, George Steinbrenner, Billy Martin, Reggie Jackson, and Thurman Munson, many of them one-on-one talks, and with the supporting cast, Sparky Lyle, Rick Cerone, Bucky Dent, Paul Blair, Mike Torrez, and Fran Healy.

To fill in the gaps of games and events I did not cover, and what transpired after I left the beat in 1983, I leaned heavily on the writings of others (see the bibliography), most notably *Damned Yankees* by Bill Madden and Moss Klein and *The Bronx Is Burning* by Jonathan Mahler. I used them to double-check my dates and to make certain I hadn't omitted anything.

I also recalled interviews that may have appeared in part in my previously published books: *BillyBall* with Billy Martin, *My Favorite Summer 1956* with Mickey Mantle, *Slick: My Life in and around Baseball* with Whitey Ford, and *Talkin' Baseball: An Oral History of Baseball in the 1970s.*

I am indebted to Billy Martin Jr. and Judge Eddie Sapir, who gave generously of their time to speak lovingly of Billy Martin as father, client, and friend.

Preface

I have known Billy Martin Jr. since he was nine years old and I am proud that, all these years later, he and my son, Dave, are partners in Pro Agents, Inc., representing baseball players. Billy's father would have liked that.

From Mickey Mantle, Whitey Ford, Hank Bauer, and Bill "Moose" Skowron, I gleaned stories of Billy Martin as a player, teammate, and running mate.

Rod Carew talked fondly about Billy Martin as a coach and manager of the Minnesota Twins and of Martin's support and faith as a mentor and surrogate father.

Mickey Morabito, director of public relations for the Yankees during Martin's tenure as manager, was as close to him as anyone and provided insight into Martin as a manager and a man.

My own relationship with both George Steinbrenner and Billy Martin—and to a lesser extent Reggie Jackson and Thurman Munson—ran the gamut from that of adversary, which was inherent in our respective positions, reporter vis-a-vis news source, to sounding board, counselor, and occasional adviser. I trust I discharged my responsibility delicately while doing my job without antagonizing any of them.

I am grateful to Robert Wilson, who conceived the idea for this book, and to the good people at Globe Pequot Press/Lyons Press for their diligence in making this idea become a reality: to Tom McCarthy and Jeff Serena for their encouragement, and especially to Shelley Wolf for her support, her dedication, and her hard work.

I'd like to thank Angela Troisi of the *New York Daily News*, Patricia Kelly at the National Baseball Hall of Fame Library, and Billy Martin Jr. for their assistance in gathering photos for this book.

Preface

I owe a debt of gratitude to the *New York Daily News* for entrusting me with the assignment of covering the most important, most prestigious, and most successful franchise in sports during this historic time. Covering the Yankees, "The Bronx Zoo," in that wild and wacky period was a rare experience. It also was a privilege just as rare.

—*Phil Pepe*
Englewood, New Jersey

Introduction

On a sultry and overcast morning in May 2007, just a few days before what would have been his father's 79th birthday, 42-year-old Billy Martin Jr., now a father himself, traveled north on the Major Deegan Expressway, past Yankee Stadium, past Yonkers Raceway, onto the Sprain Brook Parkway, to the Taconic State Parkway, and arrived in Hawthorne, New York. There Billy Martin, the elder, is laid to rest at the Gate of Heaven Cemetery, which could rightfully be called the "Cemetery to the Stars."

Gate of Heaven is the final resting place of former New York City mayor Jimmy Walker; actors James Cagney, Fred Allen, Anna Held, and Sal Mineo; journalists Westbrook Pegler, Heywood Broun, and Dorothy Kilgallen; union leader Mike Quill; former New York Football Giants owner Wellington Mara; mobster Dutch Schultz; and baseball's greatest personality, Babe Ruth.

Billy Martin Jr., having come from his home in Arlington, Texas, made the 22-mile journey from midtown Manhattan that would bring back a flood of memories. He had not visited his father's gravesite since the burial some 17½ years earlier, a day, he said, "that's all a blur now. I always wanted to come back, but I thought it was a lot farther from the city than it is. Now that I know how close it is, I plan to come back often when I'm in New York."

Introduction

High atop a hill that sits about two pitchers' mounds distance from the grave of the incomparable Babe Ruth is Martin's simple but elegant tombstone, about 6 feet wide, with the numeral 1 etched on either side. Engraved under the 1 on the left side are the words Forever #1. To the right of the numeral 1 is an engraving of a saint, under which are the words St. Jude Pray For Us.

Under the numeral 1 on the right it reads Until We Meet Again. To the left of the numeral 1 is this epitaph: "I may not have been the greatest Yankee to put on the uniform, but I was the proudest. B.M."

In the center is a huge crucifix under which is the name Martin. Below the crucifix, the inscription is as follows:

Alfred Manuel
"Billy"
May 16, 1928
December 25, 1989

On top of the headstone on that day were several rocks and coins, two casino chips, and a yellowed, weathered piece of paper that clearly had been left there some years before. Printed on the paper was a prayer and the words "Wayside Elementary School, Ocean Township School District #3870."

Billy Martin Jr., called Billy Joe by his father, solemnly approached the gravesite, gently placed flowers at the foot of the headstone, and talked lovingly of his father and of his final resting place.

"Mr. Steinbrenner made the arrangements for the funeral at St. Patrick's Cathedral and for the burial here and paid for Dad's coffin," he said. "For that, I am very grateful. Wife No. 4 [Jill Guiver] asked me what I thought about Dad being buried here. It was either here or back in California near his mother. She said she found a place where Dad could be buried near Babe Ruth. To me that was a no-brainer because the star shone the brightest here. I give her credit for that, and for asking me my opinion and letting me have some input on what went on the headstone."

It was Billy Joe who suggested the line "Until We Meet Again" and also the inclusion of St. Jude.

"Contrary to what most people probably think, my father was a very spiritual man," said Billy Jr. "He wore a cross on his baseball cap. He always went to church. Whenever I was with him and we'd go to the ballpark, on the way we'd stop at a church. If we got there 10 minutes before Mass started, we'd sit and wait. If it was 10 minutes after Mass started or with 10 minutes left to the Mass, we'd wait until Mass ended. If there wasn't a service for a couple of hours, we'd just sit there and pray.

"St. Jude was Dad's favorite saint."

The patron saint for hopeless causes, he was told.

"Isn't that appropriate?" Billy Jr. said.

"This site is neat because Dad had a thing about Babe Ruth. He never asked questions about players, but he always asked questions about Babe Ruth. He often asked Pete Sheehy [New York's longtime clubhouse custodian, who went back to Ruth's day] about the Babe. There's a restaurant in New Jersey near where Dad lived. It's called Steve's Sizzling Steaks, and Dad liked the food there and he liked hanging out there. The owner, Steve, knew Babe Ruth. There are a lot of pictures of celebrities in the restaurant, but behind the bar, in the most prominent place in the restaurant, there are only two pictures, one of Babe Ruth and the other of Dad. Not too long ago, I stopped in the restaurant, and Steve bought me a shot of Royal Salut. 'That's what your dad liked,' he said."

The last time Billy Jr. saw his father was at the funeral of his grandmother just two weeks before the elder Billy was killed in an automobile accident at the age of 61. Billy Jr. was only 24 at the time.

"It's a sad thing to say," said Billy Jr., "but in a way I'm grateful that his mother died before Dad. A mother shouldn't be alive to see her son buried. On a personal level, my grandmother's death allowed Dad and me some closure on what was a real uncomfortable time for us. For about six months, we hardly talked, and that wasn't like us. Until then, we used to talk all the time. When I saw him at his mother's funeral, it had been the longest we had ever gone without seeing one another.

"I was finishing college at Texas Tech and I had to go to summer school to get my degree. I had to pay my own tuition for my last three semesters because my tuition payments were not being made as Dad thought they were. He was told that the money was sent, but that I was using it for other things: that I was spending it on drugs and that I was a hippie and a party animal. That wasn't the truth, but I figured Dad believed it because when I called him and left messages, I wouldn't hear back from him. I found out later that he never got my messages.

"When my grandmother died, Dad was told that I didn't want to go to the funeral, that I was having too much fun in college. Another untruth. I couldn't get through to him, so I made my own arrangements and flew to Berkeley for the funeral. I brought my diploma with me. You should have seen the look of surprise on his face when I walked into the hotel where he was staying.

He said he expected me to have long hair and a beard and to be dressed like a beatnik.

"Dad's friend Bill Reedy was there, and he said to Dad, 'Billy, we need to go have a drink.'

"I wanted to put my bags in my room first, so I told them I'd meet them in the hotel bar in a few minutes. Bill Reedy took me aside and said, 'Bring your diploma with you.'

"I went to my room, dropped off my bags, and joined them at the hotel bar, carrying my diploma. When I showed it to Dad, he couldn't talk. I was the first member of our family to graduate from college, and Dad was so proud. He also was angry that he had been duped. He was about to explode. He just sat there seething for a long time without talking. It was not like my father not to talk. I think he felt bad that he never discussed it with me, because I had never lied to him about anything, and here he was led to believe that I had lied about what I did with the tuition money he thought I was getting all along.

"As sad as it was that my grandmother died, I'm grateful the way things turned out, because if she had not died when she did, I might not have seen my dad, and he would have died thinking I had squandered the tuition money. That would have been hard for me to live with."

Having resolved his differences with his father, Billy Jr. was looking forward to spending time with him soon after Christmas Day, 1989.

"It was all arranged. I would go to his home in upstate New York, and then we'd fly together to California," Billy Jr. remembered. "Dad had friends in Newport Beach and at the Balboa Bay Club, and we were going to meet up with them for New Year's and then go to Mexico on a hunting trip."

Before departing for upstate New York, Billy Jr. planned to have Christmas dinner with his mother, Gretchen Martin, at the home of her fiancé in Arlington, Texas.

"On Christmas night, my mom got a telephone call from one of her college sorority sisters. I could tell by the look on her face and the way she was talking that something was wrong. When she hung up the phone, she told me my dad had just died in a car accident. It was the worst feeling I ever had in my life, like somebody had just punched me in the pit of my stomach. Christmas will never be the same for me again.

"We didn't have the radio or television on, so it was several hours after he died that we heard about it. There were no cell phones in those days and my mom's sorority sister was one of the few people who knew where to reach her.

"My mom drove me home, and when we got there, some of my friends were sitting outside my house, waiting for me. They all knew about the accident long before I did. Our answering machine at home was full of calls from friends, but nobody was there to receive them.

"So many people have asked who was driving. Was Dad driving? Was Bill Reedy driving? [Reedy survived the accident with minor injuries and later told authorities that he was the driver. He was charged with DUI.] Whether Dad was driving or Bill was driving, God decided it was time. It was an icy road; they took the turn and slid right into the embankment of Dad's driveway. His death was almost instantaneous, but it was death nonetheless.

"There was drinking, there's no doubt about that. A lot of people are quick to judge and point fingers. Alcoholic! Drinking problem! Was Dad an alcoholic? I don't know; I'm not an expert on such things. He certainly drank, and he drank a lot. I think people need to look at things. When Dad and Mickey Mantle were playing in the '50s, watch a movie from that era. The star of the movie has a cigarette in one hand and a drink in the other, and it wasn't just considered acceptable behavior; it was cool, it was posh, it was in vogue, it was the thing to do.

"My father should be remembered for being pugnacious, a scrapper, a battler, and a tough guy. But he should also be remembered as somebody who was compassionate and who was infinitely loyal, who believed loyalty was one of the dying traits in this game and in this world."

Billy Martin's funeral was held at St. Patrick's Cathedral on Friday, December 29, 1989. The huge church was crowded to overflowing with friends, former teammates, and dignitaries in and out of baseball. John Cardinal O'Connor officiated at the service and eulogized the former Yankees manager. George Steinbrenner wept openly.

After listening to his father being eulogized, Billy Jr. sadly joined the procession leaving the church.

"My memories of my father's funeral are very gray, a lack of color in them," he recalled. "As the procession left St. Patrick's Cathedral, I started to lose it. I was convulsing into tears and sobs. Just then a man got up and grabbed my arm, steadied me, and walked me outside. He said, 'I want you to see how many people loved your father.'" We walked outside, and you couldn't even see the sidewalk; there were people everywhere, on the street, on the sidewalks, with signs and banners that said, WE LOVE YOU BILLY, and pictures of Dad with halos above his head. People have told me they tried to go to the funeral, but they couldn't get near the church, it was so crowded.

"The man who took me outside was President Richard Nixon."

At the time of his death, Billy Martin had been out of baseball a little more than a year, but there were signs he was getting ready for a return. He had received overtures to go to Japan to head up a new franchise. There was talk that some Colorado businessmen who were going to run a National League expansion franchise wanted him as their manager. And there were rumors of a Billy Martin VI with the Yankees, who had not been to the postseason in eight years and had finished that season in fifth place with a record of 74–87, 14½ games out of first place.

"Dad had a lot in the works at the time," said Billy Jr. "I don't think the Japan deal really interested him, but he was willing to listen to what they had to offer.

"The Colorado thing would have been hard for him to pass up because his first managing job was in Denver for the minor league Bears, and he still had a lot of friends there. It would have been his first managing job in the National League. He would have done what Buck Showalter did in Arizona—be involved with everything from the ground floor, player personnel, team logos and uniforms, field dimensions—and he wouldn't lose a game for two years." (The Colorado Rockies would begin play in the 1993 season.)

"Colorado would have been an ideal situation for him. But there also was talk that George Steinbrenner wanted him back with the Yankees. Knowing Dad's love for the Yankees, I think that's probably what he would have chosen. He always said he was a Yankee, and he would be a Yankee forever."

A young Billy Martin fulfilled a childhood dream when he became a New York Yankee in 1950. COURTESY BILLY MARTIN JR. COLLECTION

One

COLLISION COURSE

The voice coming through the telephone receiver on a hot and humid July afternoon in 1975 was loud and clear and unmistakably familiar. I had heard it dozens of times in similar circumstances over the previous two years. The phone would ring, I'd pick it up, and all I would hear were two words:

"It's George."

No "Hello, how are you?" No last name. Just "It's George."

George who? Axelrod? Zuverink? Burns? Brett? Marshall? Carlin?

Simply "It's George," and that could mean only one thing: George M. Steinbrenner, principal owner of the New York Yankees was on the phone, returning my call or calling unsolicited because he had something on his mind, usually a complaint about one of his players, or his manager, or his general manager, and he wanted—needed—to get it off his chest, or to plant a seed he knew would end up in the next day's newspaper.

At the time, Steinbrenner was under suspension from baseball. On April 5, 1974, the day before the Yankees were scheduled to open the season against the Indians in Cleveland, Steinbrenner had been indicted by a federal grand jury on 14 felony counts in connection with illegal campaign contributions by his American

1

Shipbuilding Company to CREEP, Richard Nixon's Committee to Re-elect the President. In an effort to keep the Yankees out of the scandal, Steinbrenner voluntarily removed himself from the daily affairs of the team, pending further investigation. That investigation led to Steinbrenner's being suspended by Commissioner Bowie Kuhn for two years, commencing November 27.

Steinbrenner was probably violating the terms of that suspension by merely making the phone call. That was not my problem. Besides, Steinbrenner said nothing for attribution.

As the writer assigned to cover the Yankees for the *Daily News,* the newspaper with New York's largest circulation, I was a favored, and frequent, recipient of those telephone calls in the early days of Steinbrenner's reign.

I had never even heard the name George M. Steinbrenner until the afternoon of January 3, 1973, when I was among the members of the media summoned to Yankee Stadium for a "major announcement," the sale of the New York Yankees by the Columbia Broadcasting System to a group headed by George M. Steinbrenner III, a shipbuilder from Lorain, Ohio. The price for baseball's most prestigious and most successful franchise was $10 million, $3 million less than CBS had paid for it eight years earlier. Steinbrenner and Michael Burke, who had been designated by CBS to run the Yankees as president and chairman of the board, would be general partners.

Who, I wondered, was this stranger from a Cleveland suburb, heading up the group that purchased baseball's most famous team? After the press conference, I returned to the office of the *Daily News* and visited the paper's library, or "morgue," in newspaper jargon. I asked the librarian to find everything he had on file under the name George M. Steinbrenner III.

I was handed a small manila envelope in which there were two clippings, one announcing that George M. Steinbrenner III, president of American Shipbuilding, had been named by *Cleveland Magazine* one of the 50 young "movers and shakers" in the United States, the other that Senator Ted Kennedy had flown to the 1972 Democratic National Convention in Miami on a plane chartered by Ohio shipbuilding magnate George M. Steinbrenner III.

Less than six years later, it would take a shopping cart to carry all the clippings about the Yankees owner. Steinbrenner clearly liked seeing his name in the newspapers and understood the value of publicity better than most.

In the spring of 1975, a friend of Catfish Hunter informed me that a simple blood test revealed that the Yankees star pitcher had diabetes and was under treatment for the disease. I wrote the story for the *Daily News,* which ran it on the tabloid's back page.

When Steinbrenner heard what I had written, he was irate. He confronted me and asked how I could write something that was so destructive to his team, that could cause a distraction and give aid and comfort to the enemy. I patiently lectured Steinbrenner on the rudiments of Journalism 101. I told him I didn't work for the Yankees. I owed them nothing. My obligation was to my newspaper and its readers.

George seemed mollified by my explanation.

"Well," he demurred, "at least we got the back page."

One week after the purchase of the Yankees was announced, another press conference was held in New York's posh "21" Club, where the limited partners of Steinbrenner's group were introduced. Among them was Gabe Paul, a longtime baseball executive whose career had begun in 1926 when, at the age of 16, he was public-ity director and ticket manager for Rochester of the International

League. He would rise to become general manager and president of the Cincinnati Reds and, later, the Cleveland Indians, where he befriended a young George Steinbrenner. It was Paul who learned from Mike Burke that CBS might be looking to sell the Yankees, and he brought that information to Steinbrenner's attention.

"Wow, I thought," Steinbrenner recalled. "To a young man [he was 42 at the time], owning the New York Yankees, or even a piece of them, was beyond belief.

"I went to New York, and I met with Mr. Paley [William S. Paley, president and chairman of the board of CBS]. I walked into his office, and he was looking out the window. At first, he didn't even look at me, and then he wheeled around and said, 'Are you here with Chinese paper?'

"I said, 'No, sir, I'm here with all the money that I could get together at this time. This is it. I'd like to buy them.'

"He said, 'You got a deal.'

"I almost fell out of the chair. At that point, the Yankees weren't doing so well, on the field or at the gate. To Paley's credit, it was one of the best deals I ever made because everything he promised me, he honored. If somebody said, 'Let's do this,' he said, 'No, I made my promise to him.' And that's the way it was."

As his finder's fee, Gabe Paul was brought along to New York with Steinbrenner as a limited partner with the title director of special projects.

The inclusion of Paul in the new ownership group raised suspicions. Six weeks earlier, acting as operative for the Indians, Paul had traded the coveted, power-hitting, left-handed swinging third baseman Graig Nettles to the Yankees for four young prospects, a deal that brought charges of impropriety in baseball circles.

What's more, if Burke were to continue as president and CEO of the Yankees, and Lee MacPhail were to continue as the team's general manager, what function was Paul to perform?

Addressing the question, Burke suggested that Paul, nearing age 65, would serve as an observer and consultant.

"This is a nice way for Gabe to wind down his long, illustrious baseball career," said Burke.

It was at the January 3, 1973 press conference that Steinbrenner made the comment that would be hurled back at him many times over the next two decades:

"We plan absentee ownership," he said. "We're not going to pretend we're something we aren't. I'll stick to building ships and let the baseball people run the team. I won't be active in the day-to-day operation of the club at all. I can't spread myself so thin. I've got enough headaches with my shipbuilding company."

Yeah, George; right.

"Oh, boy, when I made that statement the press really took me to pieces," Steinbrenner said some years later. "There were certain writers who were against me. Here was this guy from Cleveland, and he's buying the New York Yankees. It was kind of scary. To think that the greatest team in the history of all organized sports, and here's this young guy telling us what he's going to do—I had promised I would deliver a championship within four years. We bought the team in 1973, and four years later we were world champions, so we did what we said we'd do."

Did George M. Steinbrenner III make good on his promise to bring back the championship years to the New York Yankees and make the Yankee name even greater than it was? You be the judge.

In the eight years before CBS assumed ownership, the New York Yankees won seven pennants and three World Series and never drew fewer than 1.3 million customers to Yankee Stadium.

In the eight years under CBS's ownership, the Yankees won no championships, finished higher than fourth once, and never drew as many as 1.3 million customers to Yankee Stadium, falling to a low of 966,328 in 1972.

In the first eight years of George Steinbrenner's ownership, the Yankees won four American League East titles, three pennants, two World Series, and surpassed two million in home attendance five times, with a high of 2.6 million in 1980.

Since then, under the stewardship of Steinbrenner, who has owned the team longer than any other Yankees owner, they have won four more world championships and reached the once unthinkable total of four million in home attendance.

It didn't take long for Steinbrenner to renege on his promise to "stick to building ships" and stay out of the day-to-day operation of the ballclub, or for a power struggle to develop between him and Burke.

That spring, Steinbrenner arrived in Fort Lauderdale and roamed the field with a pen and pad on which he wrote notes for delivery to manager Ralph Houk.

"Tell No. 14, No. 26, and No. 36 to get a haircut.

"No. 15 is wearing his hat backwards."

"George," Houk replied, "he's a catcher. Catchers wear their hats backwards."

George Steinbrenner was among the first of a new breed of baseball owner. In the past, owners were seen but rarely heard. They were paternalistic like Tom Yawkey with the Boston Red Sox and Horace Stoneham with the New York Giants, or like Philip K. Wrigley with the Chicago Cubs and Dan Topping with the New York Yankees, they remained in the background, took care of their other businesses, clipped coupons, and let the baseball people run their teams. Then along came the mavericks, Bill Veeck with the St. Louis Browns, Charles O. Finley with the Kansas City Athletics, and George Steinbrenner with the Yankees, who were involved, hands-on owners.

"I had never played the game of baseball," Steinbrenner would say in later years. "I didn't know. I was in a situation where all these veterans that were great players, all the managers and coaches I had, didn't understand what I was talking about when I talked about focus and discipline.

"Howard Cosell used to call me 'Patton in pinstripes.' Maybe I am that way. Maybe I am that way too much, but that's the way I am, and if you want to play for me, if you want to march in my army, that's the way you have to march. I take the responsibility for all I've done wrong, but I feel I do know how teams must play to win and how people connected with that team, with the organization, must be disciplined and focused. What they do with

7

their private lives, that's another thing. If I can ever help them in any way, I usually do. But I want them to be focused on their one objective.

"What was it Douglas MacArthur said? The hope of victory is essential I want them to feel that way."

One day during his first spring training, Steinbrenner felt that as the new leader of the Yankees, it was incumbent upon him to address the team and lay down some rules.

"I made my usual locker room speech, which could easily, possibly have been done without in those days," he said. "But I gave it anyway, about the pride of the Yankees and you've got to do this and you've got to do that, and about the haircuts and the neatness: 'I don't want to see a softball team from Podunk out there, I want to see the New York Yankees. You'll wear your uniforms a certain way, and you won't wear your caps backwards unless you're a catcher.'

"Piniella raised his hand and said, 'I got a question.'

"'Yeah, Lou,' I said. 'What is it?' I knew it was coming because there's Sparky Lyle sitting right next to him, and he was whispering in his ear.

"Lou said, 'I was always taught that the way you wear your hair doesn't make any difference. Jesus wore his hair right down to his shoulders.' And Lou really had long hair in those days.

"I said, 'You know, you're right, Piniella.' I was trying to think of what to say to him. I said, 'Come on up here in the front of the room. We'll just have a little test here. What's that?'

"'That's the stadium,' Lou said. And that was pretty good for him.

"'And what's that?'

"'That's the high school stadium.'

"'What's that over there, Lou?'

"He said, 'That's the swimming pool of the superintendent that takes care of the grounds.'

"I said, 'Well, the day you can go over there and walk across the pool, you can wear your hair any way you want.'"

George Steinbrenner had hardly settled in and gotten used to the idea of being the owner of sport's most prestigious team when he was shocked, and the team was rocked, by a story that would set the tone for the Steinbrenner regime. Although the Steinbrenner era would be fraught with wackiness and controversy, this was one event that not only was not of his making, it was one of which he had no knowledge.

Spring training was only days old when president Mike Burke, general manager Lee MacPhail, and manager Ralph Houk invited the reporters covering the team into the manager's office in Fort Lauderdale Stadium and proceeded to stun the assembled media with a story so bizarre as to defy belief.

Two members of the Yankees pitching staff, Fritz Peterson, who had won 20 games in 1970 and 69 games over the past four seasons, and Mike Kekich, who had begun to fulfill his great promise by winning 10 games in each of the previous two years—both left-handers, such close friends that they were practically inseparable—had entered into an arrangement whereby they would trade wives. Not just wives, but children, family pets, and residences.

Peterson would move in with Kekich's wife and children in the Kekich home, Kekich would move in with Peterson's wife and children in the Peterson home. Their intention, agreed to by their spouses, was for each couple to obtain a divorce and marry each other's spouses.

Steinbrenner was so stunned by this revelation, for the first time—and the last—he was rendered speechless.

Michael Burke was a renaissance man and the anti-Steinbrenner. Suave, urbane, flamboyant, and charming, his clothes were of the latest cut, and he wore his gray hair styled in the fashion of the day, long enough that it likely would not meet with Steinbrenner's approval if Burke played for the Yankees.

Burke had been an outstanding halfback at the University of Pennsylvania, and he had an impressive war record. During World War II, he served with the Office of Strategic Services, the predecessor of the CIA. He was portrayed in the movie *Cloak and Dagger* by Gary Cooper, the same actor who starred as Lou Gehrig in George Steinbrenner's favorite movie, *The Pride of the Yankees.*

That was the only thing Burke and Steinbrenner had in common. Burke knew little about baseball and less about running a baseball team, but he came to enjoy his position as president of the New York Yankees and to cherish its glamour, excitement, and high visibility. It was for those reasons that it seemed inevitable that Burke and Steinbrenner would clash.

The season was not a month old when Steinbrenner announced that Burke had "decided" to resign his post as Yankees president and remain as a consultant. Gabe Paul would be the new team president, and the Yankees would have one general partner, George M. Steinbrenner III. Burke, standing at Steinbrenner's side, made no comment.

"A lot of times, making someone a consultant is putting him out to pasture or a settlement," Steinbrenner said. "This isn't the case here."

But in the weeks that followed, Burke, who had been a constant presence at Yankee Stadium—in the press box, on the field before games, in the clubhouse—was conspicuous by his absence and out of the picture. Soon to follow would be MacPhail and the team's longtime and gifted director of public relations, Bob Fishel. Meanwhile, manager Houk was growing wary of interference from his new owner, who began spending more and more time with the team to the dismay of the manager and his players.

In June, Steinbrenner showed up in Texas for a series against the Rangers and was seated in a box alongside the New York dugout on the third base side. The Yankees shortstop was Gene Michael, who had a well-known aversion to insects and other objects, animate and inanimate, that crawl, ooze, or slime, a phobia often exploited by his more playful teammates.

"While we were batting," Michael recalled, "Hal Lanier [another Yankees infielder] put half of a hot dog in one of the fingers of my glove. When our inning was over, I went out to my position, put on my glove, and felt something slimy in there. I shook my glove, and nothing came out. I shook it again, and a piece of hot dog came out, so I took the hot dog and fired it past the dugout, but it slid over in front of a security cop who was sitting on a wooden chair right in front of George Steinbrenner."

Steinbrenner asked the security cop for the hot dog and kept it until the end of the game, when he carried it to Houk's office.

He told his manager what had occurred and ordered him to "find out who did this and punish the man."

Houk, a rugged Kansan who was known as "The Major" and had earned a battlefield commission during World War II, ruled his team with fear and intimidation but was regarded as a players' manager who would not abide meddling from above. He simply ignored Steinbrenner's order.

In August, Steinbrenner again joined the team during a visit to Texas. He watched his Yankees get belted by the Rangers, 8–1. After the game, he telephoned Houk in his room.

"Get rid of Callison," George ordered.

Johnny Callison had enjoyed a productive 16-year major league career, mostly with the Philadelphia Phillies, but it was clear, even to a baseball novice, that he was coming to the end.

"We can't get rid of Callison," Houk protested. "Besides, we've only got about a month to go, and we're going to have to pay him anyway. And in a couple of days you can expand the roster, so there's no reason to get rid of him now."

"You go tell him he's gone," Steinbrenner persisted.

"I decided I wouldn't do that," Houk said years later. "I called Lee MacPhail and I said, 'Lee, I'm not going to tell Callison he's gone. I'm just not going to do it.'"

"Let me talk to him [Steinbrenner]," MacPhail suggested.

A few minutes later, MacPhail called Houk and said, "You better tell Callison he's gone."

To Houk, more perceptive than most, the writing was clearly on the wall, and it was in the fine hand of George Steinbrenner. Houk had signed with the Yankees as a 19-year-old, and for 34 years, as a player, minor league manager, major league coach, major league manager, and general manager, the Yankees were the only organization he knew. After piloting them to American League pennants in 1961, '62, and '63, and World Series victories in 1961 and '62, he had purchased a cabin cruiser that he dubbed *ThanksYanks*. But now he knew he could go on no longer.

After the final game of the season, Houk gathered his players around him in the clubhouse. Fighting back tears, the seemingly unflappable Major told his team, "I'm handing in my resignation."

Some years later, Houk denied he left the Yankees because of Steinbrenner.

"That really wasn't true," Houk claimed. "That was his first year as owner, and he really didn't bother me at all except a little bit toward the end when he decided we were going to change coaches. I argued about that because I always felt you had to have your own coaches as a manager. That started a little disagreement there.

"I had been in New York a long time, and we were having a rough time We weren't winning ballgames. The losing and all the other stuff just got to me, the crowds screaming and hollering at me as they do, which is normal in New York, or any baseball city. But I think it's especially true in New York.

"I discussed it with my wife, Betty, and we said maybe we'll retire.

"I still had a year to go on my contract, and George tried to get me to stay. The fact is he was quite honest with me. He said, 'Ralph, you're going to make a mistake if you leave here. I'm going to go out and get some good ballplayers; I'm going to pay for them.' At the time, I really didn't know George that well, and I thought, 'Well, that's probably a lot of talk.' But he did. He went out and he got Reggie Jackson, he got Catfish Hunter, and that's what won him those pennants, the money he spent. But at the time, I just thought it was time to get out."

"When I started," Steinbrenner said, "I was a very tough boss because I didn't understand a lot of the things you should understand if you're going to be the boss. I was young. I was not the best boss in the world. I was an impatient boss. I was very demanding—I'm still demanding, I'm still disciplined, I still insist on those same things, but now I try to say if I'm insisting on those things, I've got to give something back. And that's what I try to do."

Observed Bob Watson, one of Steinbrenner's seemingly endless string of general managers: "If things go right, they're his team. If things go wrong, they're your team. His line is, 'I will never have a heart attack. I give them.'"

Two weeks after Houk resigned from the Yankees, Dick Williams, manager of the Oakland Athletics, held a team meeting prior to Game 3 of the World Series between Oakland and the New York Mets and stunned his players by telling them he would submit his resignation after the Series. Williams had won a pennant as manager of the Boston Red Sox in 1967 and three consecutive pennants with Oakland in 1971, '72, and '73, but he had had his fill of Oakland's tempestuous owner, Charlie Finley.

"I've had it," Williams told his troops. "I'm going to quit at the end of the World Series, regardless of what happens."

True to his word, Williams announced his resignation minutes after the final out of the seventh game that nailed down

Oakland's second straight World Series victory and walked off the job with two years remaining on his contract.

Steinbrenner moved quickly to sign Williams and bring him to New York as a replacement for Houk. A press conference to introduce Williams as the new manager of the Yankees was held at a restaurant near Shea Stadium, which would be the Bombers' temporary home for the 1974 and '75 seasons while Yankee Stadium was undergoing renovation.

It presumably escaped Steinbrenner's notice that Williams was still under contract to Oakland, but it did not escape Finley's. Never one to stand in a man's way—or to let an opportunity pass to get the upper hand on a fellow owner—Finley magnanimously said he would release Williams from his contract on the condition that the Yankees compensate him with two young players, Scott McGregor, a 20-year-old left-handed pitcher who had been New York's number one pick in the June 1972 free agent draft, and Otoniel "Otto" Vélez, a 23-year-old outfielder from Puerto Rico who that season had hit 29 home runs and driven in 98 runs for AAA Syracuse.

The Yankees refused to submit to Finley's demands.

"We're not going to mortgage our future," said Yankees president Gabe Paul. "McGregor and Vélez are our crown jewels, and we're not going to give them up."

(Paul's boast of Vélez's and McGregor's worth to New York proved overblown. In four seasons with the Yankees, Vélez had 6 home runs and 28 RBI and never batted higher than .266. He went to Toronto in the 1976 expansion draft and had a mediocre 11-year career in which he batted .251 with 78 home runs and 272 RBI. McGregor never pitched a game for the Yankees. He was dealt to Baltimore in a spectacular nine-player trade midway in the 1976 season. In Baltimore, he became a star, posting double figures in wins for nine straight seasons, including 20 wins in 1980. He finished with a record of 138–108 and helped the Orioles win two American League pennants and one World Series.)

Finley remained steadfast in his demand, but the Yankees remained just as steadfast in their refusal. They gave up on signing Williams and began the search for another manager.

To fill the vacancy, the Yankees settled on Bill Virdon. Although he had spent his entire career in the National League, Virdon was not without a Yankee connection. Originally signed by the Yankees, he never made it to the Bronx, but was traded out of their minor league system to the St. Louis Cardinals in 1954 for veteran outfielder Enos Slaughter. The Cardinals, in turn, traded Virdon to the Pittsburgh Pirates in 1956, and four years later he was the regular center fielder for the Pirates when they defeated the Yankees in the 1960 World Series.

It was, in fact, a ground ball by Virdon in the eighth inning of the seventh game of the 1960 World Series with the Pirates trailing 7–4 that hit a pebble, jumped up, and caught Yankees shortstop Tony Kubek in the Adam's apple. That opened the gates for the Pirates to score five runs, then eventually win the climactic game and the Series, on Bill Mazeroski's dramatic home run in the bottom of the ninth.

After retiring as a player in 1968, Virdon served as a coach for the Pirates until 1972, when he was named to replace Danny Murtaugh as the team's manager. In his first season, Virdon led the Pirates to a division title but lost to the Cincinnati Reds in the National League Championship Series.

With the Pirates a disappointing third in September 1973, Virdon was fired and replaced by the man he had succeeded, Murtaugh.

Still eager to manage, Virdon accepted a job with Denver in the AAA American Association for the 1974 season, but when the Yankees called, Virdon was allowed out of his Denver contract so that he could manage the Yankees.

A stickler for physical fitness, Virdon's penchant for running a tight and rigorous camp in spring training quickly earned the approval of his boss, Steinbrenner, but not his players.

"I never ran so much in my life," moaned outfielder Lou Piniella.

Virdon inherited a team that had finished fourth in the American League East in 1973 with a record of 80–82, but with several new faces, most notably Piniella, who had been obtained in a trade with Kansas City, and Chris Chambliss, who came in a trade with Cleveland, the Yankees battled the Baltimore Orioles for the American League East championship right down to the final weekend of the season.

On September 4, the Yankees beat Milwaukee, 3–0, and moved into first place, where they would remain until dropping a doubleheader against the Red Sox 20 days later. As they headed to Milwaukee for the final two days of the season on October 1, the Yankees were only one game behind the Orioles.

On the airplane flight carrying the Yankees from New York to Milwaukee, backup players Rick Dempsey and Bill Sudakis engaged in a scuffle that began with typical player bantering. Their teammates quickly separated the two players before the incident escalated, but when the team arrived at the Pfister Hotel, the bantering continued in the hotel lobby. Soon, punches were thrown, and Dempsey and Sudakis were rolling around on the lobby floor. Veteran Bobby Murcer, acting as a peacemaker, jumped into the fray to break up the scuffle, but in the melee,

Murcer's finger was stepped on and broken, sidelining him for the final two games.

Murcer had been the team's leading run producer, and his bat was missed as the Yankees lost the first game of the series to the Brewers, 3–2 in 10 innings, thereby eliminating them from title contention. Nevertheless, the Yankees won 89 games and finished in second place, their highest finish in 10 years, and Virdon was rewarded by being named American League Manager of the Year by *The Sporting News*. Disregarding his own decision to voluntarily absent himself from the daily affairs of the Yankees while the investigation into his alleged illegal campaign contributions was ongoing, Steinbrenner had made the trip to Milwaukee for the final two games. When the Yankees were officially eliminated, he made his way to the clubhouse, explaining, "I want to be with my players. I'm so proud of them." He embraced the players, thanked them for their effort, and promised that things were about to change.

Coincidentally, within a month of Steinbrenner's vow, Jim "Catfish" Hunter, the American League's premier pitcher who had won 25 games for the Oakland Athletics that season and 88 in four seasons, declared himself a free agent. Hunter contended that the A's had breached his contract by failing to meet a deadline by which time the team was to pay $50,000, half of his annual salary, to a life insurance fund.

On November 26, 1974, one day before Steinbrenner's two-year suspension was to take effect, Hunter and Oakland owner Charles O. Finley met in the offices of the American Arbitration Association for a hearing to resolve the dispute. Two weeks later, arbitrator Peter Seitz declared Hunter a free agent, setting in motion a bidding war that, as the start of the era of free agency, would have far-reaching consequences in baseball.

After a short moratorium, Commissioner Kuhn ruled that teams could contact and negotiate with Hunter, and they beat a path to the office of Cherry, Cherry & Flythe, Hunter's attorneys in Ahoskie, North Carolina. Every major league team, represented by its owner, general manager, or manager, and in some cases players, made a pitch to sign Hunter.

While he didn't make the trip to Ahoskie, Steinbrenner asked for, and was granted, permission from Kuhn to be involved in the negotiation to the extent that he could communicate with his representatives in order to set guidelines on terms of the Yankee offer.

In a move that was both theatric and practical, and would set the tone for Steinbrenner's administration, the Yankees called a hastily arranged press conference on New Year's Eve, some four hours before the end of 1974, at their temporary offices near Shea Stadium to announce they had won the Catfish Hunter Sweepstakes. Hunter had agreed to a five-year contract for $3.75 million, three times the salary of any other major league player and almost half as much as the group headed by Steinbrenner had paid to buy the Yankees less than two years earlier. For tax purposes, the deal was announced in the final hours of 1974.

It was a deal that clearly had George Steinbrenner's fingerprints all over it. Having served a little more than a month of his suspension, Steinbrenner had begun to make good on his promise to bring better players to the Yankees, no matter the cost.

With the signing of Hunter, expectations were high for the Yankees for 1975. However, when they started the season by losing six of their first seven games, disillusionment began to set in. By May 17, they were 12–20 and had fallen into fourth place, 7½ games out of first, but they recouped to win 33 of their next 54 games and arrived at the All-Star break in second place, just 3½ games out of first. They would win only 5 of their first 15 games after the All-Star break, however, and slip below .500 at 50–51, 11 games off the pace.

It was about that time that my telephone rang and I heard the familiar two words, "It's George."

Steinbrenner touched on many subjects during a long and rambling conversation, which, in truth, was more a monologue than a conversation. Eventually, he got around to discussing Virdon, and it was evident that Steinbrenner was none too pleased with his manager. From his comments, it seemed Steinbrenner's complaint was more a matter of style than substance.

"I don't want a manager who walks slowly to the mound with his head down to change a pitcher like he has the weight of the world on his shoulders," Steinbrenner said. "I want a manager who dashes out of the dugout and goes to the mound with confidence and purpose and waves to the bullpen to bring in a relief pitcher as if to say, 'We have a problem here, and I know exactly what I need to do to fix it.'"

I listened to Steinbrenner's words, and one thought kept running through my head: My God, he's describing Billy Martin.

Two

BASEBALL DOCTOR

In 1975, less than two years after he took over as manager of the Texas Rangers, Billy Martin was losing his grip; his job was in jeopardy. It was not an unfamiliar scenario. He had gone this route before, in Minnesota and in Detroit. This was his established pattern:

1. Billy Martin is hired to manage a ballclub.
2. Under Martin, the team quickly and dramatically improves.
3. Martin feuds with his front office and wears out his welcome.
4. Martin is fired.
5. Martin is hired by another team.
6. The process is repeated.

When his playing career ended after the 1961 season, the Minnesota Twins, the last of his seven teams, offered him a job as a major league scout. With no other prospects and a desire to stay in baseball, the one thing he knew, Martin accepted. At the time, he had given no thought to ever being a manager.

Martin scouted for three years, a job he enjoyed, free from the daily pressure to win, just enough travel for him to indulge his passion for hunting, fishing, and golf. Best of all, he was around baseball and baseball people.

When Twins manager Sam Mele asked him to be his third base coach in 1965, Martin reluctantly gave up the relatively peaceful life of a scout and returned to the field mainly because of Mele, a man he had played for, liked, and respected.

For the next three years, Martin served as Mele's third base coach and infield instructor and took particular interest in two players, a Cuban-born shortstop named Zoilo Versalles, and a young second baseman named Rodney Cline Carew, who was born in Panama and raised in New York City.

Under Martin's tutelage, Versalles batted .273, hit 19 home runs, drove in 77 runs, stole 27 bases, and was named 1965 American League Most Valuable Player as the Twins won Minnesota's first American League pennant by seven games over the Chicago White Sox.

Two seasons later, Carew, a skinny 21-year-old with a sweet left-handed swing, arrived in the Twins spring training camp. Martin took an immediate liking to him, and he to Billy.

"From the start, Billy was a big influence on me," Carew said. "Sam Mele told Billy that I was going to be his project; that he had to take me and work with me and make me into a second baseman because [Twins owner] Calvin Griffith wanted me to play.

"Billy and I got along so well. He taught me everything about playing the game. He became a mentor to me: a big brother and a dad. The one lesson I learned from him as I was working with him was do not make mistakes. We were playing an exhibition game in Atlanta, and I made a mistake. When I came into the dugout, the first thing he said to me was, 'I don't want to hear an alibi. Did you mess up? Did you make the wrong decision?'

"I said, 'Yeah.' And he said, 'That's what I want to hear. From today on, you will play the game and use your head. If you make a mistake, you make a mistake. But don't look for an excuse.'

"That's how our relationship got under way, and from then on it was a father–son type relationship." To Martin, Carew was "not only a great hitter but a kid who could run like a deer, who was willing to learn, and who took instruction beautifully."

Carew had come with something of a reputation as a bit of a problem player, one who could be a bad influence on a ballclub. He had gotten into an argument with his manager in the minor leagues, and the manager had submitted a bad report on the youngster, whose reputation preceded him to Minnesota. Martin found Carew's reputation was undeserved.

"He was a very sensitive kid," said Martin, "but one of great compassion and feeling, not to mention his burning desire and drive to be the best."

"I was a kind of quiet and moody kid," Carew admitted. "I'd get upset a lot, and Billy would tell me, 'You've got to stay on an even keel. You've got to stop bouncing up and down like a yo-yo.' I'd look at him and say, 'You have some nerve telling me that,' and Billy would just bust out laughing."

When Mele and his coaches sat down to select the 25 men who would be taken north for the start of the 1967 season, most were in favor of returning Carew to the minor leagues. Martin was the only holdout.

"I listened to what the other coaches were saying about him, and I couldn't believe they were talking about the same kid I had been working with," said Martin. "I tried to speak on his behalf, but I was talked down, so I kept quiet, and later I went to Mele.

"'Sam,' I said, 'this is a good kid, believe me. He's polite. He comes from a good family. He's quiet. And he works hard.'

"Yeah, Billy," Mele replied. "But I'm not sure he's ready to play in the big leagues."

"I know the kid, Sam," Martin insisted. "I've been working with him. He's ready."

"Mr. Griffith wanted to give me the opportunity, but all the other coaches and the farm director wanted to send me back to the minor leagues," Carew recalled. "Billy had put in so much work with me during the spring. Day in and day out, he was out there with me. He saw the progress I had made, and he was happy with my progress. He knew I was going to hit, but he wanted me to get better at my defensive skills. He stood in my corner."

Not only did Carew prove to be ready for the big leagues in 1967, in his first year he batted .292, hit 8 home runs and drove in 55 runs, and was voted American League Rookie of the Year. He would go on to get 3,053 hits, win seven batting championships, more than any American Leaguer except Ty Cobb, and have a lifetime average of .328 in a 19-year career that landed him in the Hall of Fame.

After winning the pennant in 1965, the Twins slipped to second place in 1966. When they split their first 50 games in 1967, rumors were rampant that Mele would be fired and replaced by Martin, who had done an about-face and decided he would like a shot at managing. Being back in uniform had renewed the competitive fires within him. Watching the managerial manipulations up close and personal convinced Martin that he wanted to manage. Mele was fired, but instead of Martin, owner Calvin Griffith gave the managerial reins to veteran coach Cal Ermer.

Griffith explained that Martin was being bypassed because he had no previous experience as a manager anywhere, which created a dilemma for Martin the following May. Denver, the Twins' top farm team in the class AAA American Association, had gotten off to a terrible start under manager Johnny Goryl, and Griffith asked Martin to leave Minnesota and replace Goryl.

"I was afraid that would be a one-way ticket to oblivion," Martin would say years later. "You know, out of sight, out of mind. On the other hand, I knew that if I refused to go to Denver, I might never get the chance to manage. I had to go down there and prove I could manage."

When Martin arrived in Denver, the Bears were in last place with a record of 7–22. From the start, Martin's style as a manager was the same as his style as a player—aggressive, daring, gambling, taking chances. And it worked. Under Martin, the Bears won 65 of their last 115 games.

One of Martin's players in Denver was Graig Nettles, who confessed in his autobiography, *Balls*, that it wasn't love at first sight between him and Martin.

"The first month or so I didn't like him," Nettles wrote. "To be more precise, I hated him. He yelled and screamed whenever a player made a mistake."

Nettles was on the receiving end for more than his share of Martin's wrath, but there was a method to Billy's madness. He taught players to steal bases, use the squeeze play, and bunt men around the bases. He also recognized in Nettles a player with excellent potential and the competitiveness to work hard to get better, and to win. By the end of the season, Nettles had become a Martin convert.

"When I saw the results," Nettles said, "I stopped hating Billy Martin and I began to see him for what he was: an extraordinary leader."

With the Twins in 1969, and later with the Yankees, Nettles would become one of Martin's staunchest supporters.

What Martin was able to accomplish with the Denver Bears did not go unnoticed in Minnesota, and when the Twins fell to seventh place in 1968, Cal Ermer was fired, and Martin was brought to Minnesota to manage a major league team for the first time.

The Martin magic, the swashbuckling, daring, aggressive style of baseball, picked right up in Minnesota where it had left off in Denver. With Martin calling the shots, Rod Carew, his prize pupil, set an American League record that stands to this day and tied a major league record by stealing home seven times. He also won the first of his seven batting titles with an average of .332.

"It was Billy who got me to steal home," Carew said. "We were in spring training one day and he said, 'Rod, you run good. There are going to be times when we might not be swinging the bats well. Are you averse to trying to steal home?'

"I said I wasn't, so he took me down to third base and worked with me on taking walking leads. Then he brought out different pitchers with different windups, left-handers, right-handers, and he had me time their windup, and he would tell me when to break.

"He worked with me on stealing home the whole spring. When I finally got it down, he said, 'OK, we're going to use this as a surprise in the late innings to try to tie a ballgame or win a ballgame or put us one run down.' It became a daring thing for me. I enjoyed doing it. When I got on third base, I would look over at Billy in the dugout, and if he opened his palms, that meant I had to get a jump and try to steal home."

Under their daring rookie manager, Martin, the Twins, who had won 79 games the year before, won 97 games and finished 9 games ahead of Oakland in the American League West. Although Baltimore swept the Twins in the three-game American League Championship Series (the Orioles won Game 1, 4–3 in 12 innings, and Game 2, 1–0 in 11 innings), Billy Martin was on top of the world . . . and positioned for a great fall.

While Minnesotans, including Twins owner Calvin Griffith, marveled at Martin's work on the field, some, especially Griffith, were growing concerned with issues that occurred off the field. Not six weeks into his major league managerial career, Martin clashed with the Twins front office over a young pitcher named Charlie Walters. The manager had told the pitcher he was sending him to Denver, the Twins AAA affiliate. Instead, the farm director assigned Walters to AA Charlotte. Martin hit the roof. He felt it made him look like a liar to the youngster.

There also was an altercation with the Twins traveling secretary, Howard Fox, on a chartered plane, and in August, Martin raised Griffith's ire by getting into a brawl in a Detroit bar with one of his best pitchers, Dave Boswell, who landed in the hospital with a concussion.

In 1969, his only season under Martin, Boswell won 20 games. He never won more than 14 in any other season and finished his career with 68 victories.

Almost a decade after the brawl with Boswell, Martin was sitting in the visiting manager's office in Baltimore's Memorial Stadium, talking with reporters before a game against the Orioles. A knock on the door interrupted the conversation, and standing in the doorway was a large, blond-haired man in his 40s. He had the look, physique, and carriage of a former athlete.

"Hey, pard," said Martin as he rose out of his seat and walked to the door. The two men embraced and chatted briefly until the visitor excused himself and left.

"Who was that?" Martin was asked.

"Dave Boswell," said Martin. "He lives in the area."

"You mean Dave Boswell, the guy you punched out in Detroit?"

"Yeah," Martin said. "That thing in Detroit was forgotten the next day. He did a good job for me that year. He was a good guy. He just had too much to drink that night."

The final straw for Griffith came against Baltimore in the third game of the American League Championship Series. Down two games to none, Martin started right-hander Bob Miller, who had won five games for the Twins during the regular season, instead of Jim Kaat, a veteran left-hander who had won 131 games for the Twins in nine seasons, 14 of them that year.

Why Miller instead of Kaat?

"Because I'm the manager," was Martin's sarcastic explanation.

The Orioles blasted Miller out in the second inning and beat the Twins, 11–2.

While Kaat was disappointed in not being chosen to pitch Game 3 of the 1969 ALCS, he remained one of Martin's staunchest supporters.

"I loved pitching for him because he would let me pitch as long as I could until I couldn't get anybody out anymore," said Kaat. "Fatigue was never an issue. In my last start in spring training that year, I strained a groin muscle diving for a ball. Billy could see I was limping a little the next day at our preseason workout in Kansas City.

"I was scheduled to pitch the second game of the season in Kansas City, and Billy asked me if I would be able to make it to the post. I said I would. Billy said he was hoping I could give him five innings since it was my first start of the season. I pitched 11 innings and left with the score tied, 3–3. We lost, 4–3, in 17 innings.

"If Billy were managing today, he probably would do things differently. Back then, unless he thought the guy in the bullpen was better, he'd leave you in to finish what you started. He has been criticized for ruining young pitchers by overworking them. I don't know about that. I can only talk from my own experience, and he didn't ruin or abuse me."

The negative side of Martin, to Kaat, is a familiar complaint.

"I couldn't trust him," Kaat said. "I once saw him replace third base coach Vern Morgan in the middle of a game. That was very embarrassing, not only for Morgan but for everyone on the team.

"Billy would tell you one thing and do another. He was constantly second-guessing catchers on pitch selection. If he had a complaint with me, he wouldn't confront me himself, he'd send pitching coach Art Fowler to tell me what he thought.

"One time we got into a long, extra-inning game against the expansion Pilots in Seattle. I had pitched a complete game two days before, but Billy needed help, and he asked me if I could give him a few innings. I went into the game in the 14th with the score tied 6–6 and pitched three innings. We scored in the top of the 15th, and in the bottom of the 15th, Jim Pagliaroni hit a home run off me to tie it."

(The game was suspended after 16 innings and resumed the next day, the day astronauts Neil Armstrong and Buzz Aldrin landed on the moon. The Twins would go on to win it in 18 innings.)

"Billy had Fowler question my pitch selection to Pagliaroni," Kaat recalled. "That made my Dutch patience explode. I stormed into Martin's office.

"'If you want to call my pitches before I throw them, feel free to do it,'" I said. "'But don't second-guess what I threw.'

"I never had another problem with Billy after that incident. In that respect, Billy was a lot like George Steinbrenner. If you felt you were right about something and you stood your ground with them without disrespecting their authority, they would both back off and leave you alone.

"In my opinion, if Billy were secure enough to have hired coaches who he could delegate responsibility to, like a strong-willed pitching, hitting, and third base coach, he would have been as great a manager as one could possibly be."

Rick Cerone, who played for Martin with the Yankees in 1983, had similar problems with the manager and often took the brunt of his ire.

"I never really got along with Billy," Cerone said. "He was hard on catchers. Anytime a guy got a hit against us, it was the catcher's fault."

A few days after the Twins were eliminated in the 1969 American League Championship Series, Martin had driven from Minnesota to Nebraska to visit his in-laws when he got a call from Griffith.

"You won't be back next year," Griffith said.

"This is the hardest decision I have ever had to make about a manager," Griffith told the press. "You know Billy can go into a crowd and charm the hell out of you. But he ignored me. I asked him to come and see me several times, and he didn't."

The reaction to Martin's firing from fans in the Twin Cities was swift and predictable. They were outraged. They had come to appreciate and revel in Martin's managerial style, his daring, his feistiness, and his ability to transform the Twins into a winning team. They knew little of his squabbles with the front office, and cared less. His players felt betrayed by Twins management.

"Billy had stood in my corner throughout my career," Carew said. "Even when he left the Twins, I stayed in touch with him. If things were bothering me, I would call him to talk to him about it, and he would give me advice.

"When he managed against us, he used to always needle me. If I was coming to bat, he would point at his ribs as if to say he was going to have his pitcher stick one in my ribs. One day I said, 'Ahh, you wouldn't do that. You're my dad.'

"People can say whatever they want about that man, but I have nothing but good things to say about him. As far as I'm concerned, he was a great friend and a great human being with me. I even asked him to be godfather to my middle daughter, Stephanie, and he accepted."

For the first time in more than 20 years, Billy Martin was out of baseball. He spent 1970 working for a Minneapolis brewery, as a public relations representative for a radio station, and believing his managing days were over.

"Nobody will hire me," he said. "I tell the truth. Owners don't want guys who tell the truth. Calvin Griffith wanted me to go up to his office every day and tell him what I was doing on the field. The first day I went up, and he was on the phone. The second day his secretary told me he was taking a nap. There was no third day."

It wouldn't be long, however, before Martin would get another chance to manage a team in trouble, a situation in which he would find himself several times. He would become Dr. Martin, master of the quick fix.

Your baseball team is ailing? Bring in Dr. Martin. He's a panacea, a B12 shot. And he makes house calls. Take two Billy Martin tablets and call me in the morning.

Three

TIGER BY THE TAIL

While Billy Martin was out of baseball in 1970, the Detroit Tigers were in a free fall. Two years after winning 103 games and the World Series, they won 79 games and plummeted to fourth place. Their attendance tumbled from a high of 2,031,847 in 1968 to 1,501,293 in 1970. The Tigers were in need of a quick fix, so general manager Jim Campbell, against his better judgment and the warnings of several of his baseball colleagues, put in a call to Dr. Martin.

The improvement in the Tigers was immediate, and miraculous. In 1971, they won 91 games, good for second place in the American League East. The following year, they won 86 games and finished first in the AL East, a half game ahead of the Boston Red Sox. They also drew 1,892,386 fans, an increase over the previous year of almost 400,000, more than enough to pay Martin's salary of $65,000. Billy Martin had worked his trademark magic on a second team. He was also about to indulge in another Martin trademark, self-destruction.

For two years, things had gone relatively smoothly in Detroit for Martin, if you're willing to overlook the small stuff like the time in the spring of 1972 when he got into a shoving match with a fan, or when he complained to the front office about being saddled with two young players he didn't want, or when he argued with Campbell after benching Willie Horton for what Martin deemed a lack of hustle.

By his third season with the Tigers, Martin was spinning out of control.

The Willie Horton incident occurred in the spring of 1973, only weeks after George M. Steinbrenner III had purchased the Yankees.

"Willie would come late to the ballpark," Martin said. "He would skip batting practice, he missed the team picture, things like that. And Campbell was making excuses for him, letting Willie think it was all right for him to pull that stuff. I told Jim I couldn't have that on my team, and we had a meeting, the three of us.

"At the meeting, Horton was sitting right there, and Campbell was sticking up for him, trying to get me to allow Willie to get away with these little idiosyncrasies of his.

"'Hold it,' I said. 'Horton is just a player like the rest of them. He's no better than any of the others. He's going to do exactly what the rest of them do. No different. No favors.'

"'But, Billy . . .'

"'But nothing,' I said. 'Matter of fact, fuck you, Jim. I quit. Make Horton the manager.'

"And I walked out.

"It was nothing personal against Willie. I loved the guy. I even gave him a job as a coach when I managed the Yankees. But we were locking horns, and I couldn't lose control of him, or I would lose control of the rest of the team. I was just trying to help him grow up back there in Detroit, that's all. I was trying to get him out of the environment he was in in Detroit and let him know that he was just one of 25."

Martin and Campbell came to an uneasy peace over the Horton incident, and Billy reconsidered his threat to resign, but it became clear he was on a short leash.

On August 31, American League president Joe Cronin suspended Martin for three days after two Tigers pitchers were accused of throwing at hitters. On the third day of the suspension, Campbell called Martin to his office and informed the manager he was being let go. There were 19 games remaining in the 1973 season, and the Tigers were in third place.

"I like Jim Campbell," Martin would say years later. "I really do. He's an outstanding individual. I truly believe that when they brought me to Detroit, they intended to have me there for a long time. But I clashed with Campbell, and I think he may have resented my relationship with [John] Fetzer [the Tigers' multimillionaire owner who made his fortune from his radio and television empire].

"It seemed the friendlier I got with Mr. Fetzer, the more problems I had with Jim Campbell. Jim might have thought that I was looking to boost myself with Mr. Fetzer with an eye to one day taking Jim's job. If that's what he thought, that was far from the truth. I knew I wasn't cut out to run a ballclub, to deal with radio and TV rights and players' contracts and stadium operations.

"My expertise is in player evaluation, and it was there that I clashed with Campbell. They had players there who I thought were over the hill, and I told Campbell so. But he had signed a lot of those players when he was farm director, and he was reluctant to get rid of them.

"After we won our division in 1972, I knew the team was getting old, and I kept telling Campbell to do something.

"'Jim,' I said. 'These guys are over the hill. They've had it. They're gone. You have to make some trades.'

"He kept telling me we had some kids coming up through the farm system, but when I took a look at them in spring training, I didn't think they could play. Campbell kept touting Ike Blessitt and Marvin Lane. He said they were our outfielders of the future, but to me they couldn't play. Blessitt had all of five at bats in his major league career. Lane did a little better. He played parts of five seasons and got in 90 games and batted .207. And these were the so-called great kids Campbell wanted to stick me with. I knew they wouldn't make the grade, and that eventually got me fired.

"I made the mistake of telling Campbell he had problems and his star kids were bad, and he didn't like hearing it, so we got into it. But I was telling him these things for his own good as well as mine. I couldn't be a yes-man. I never have been and I never will be. It's not my style to tell people what they want to hear if it's wrong, especially if it means I was putting my job and my reputation on the line, too.

"I also made the mistake of asking Campbell for a three-year contract," Martin said. "I was looking for security because I didn't want to be the scapegoat when the team started going bad, as I knew it would. I told Campbell, 'I want three years.'

"He said, 'No, Billy, we're not doing it.'"

According to Martin, that sealed his doom in Detroit.

After Martin left, the Tigers would go 11 years before winning another division championship. To replace Martin, the Tigers hired Ralph Houk, recently resigned from the Yankees. Campbell, who refused to give Martin a three-year extension, signed Houk to a five-year contract.

Once again, Martin believed his managing days were over. In fact, he was out of work for six days. The Tigers fired Martin on September 2, and the Texas Rangers put in an SOS call to Dr. Martin on September 7, the day after they fired Whitey Herzog.

"The only reason I took the job," Martin said, "was as a favor to my good friend Bob Short, a man I admired a great deal, and a man who has always been there for me when I needed him."

Martin had become acquainted with Short when he managed the Twins. Short, a native Minnesotan, was an entrepreneur, sportsman, and political power broker. He owned the Leamington Hotel in Minneapolis, had owned the Minneapolis Lakers of the National Basketball Association, and was instrumental in moving the team to Los Angeles, where they enjoyed unparalleled success on the court and at the turnstiles. He was also the chairman of the National Democratic Committee and a close friend and protégé of former vice president Hubert H. Humphrey.

Short had dabbled in baseball as a minority owner in several teams, but he always aspired to owning his own team. His chance would come after the American League expanded to 10 teams in 1961. The Washington Senators moved to Minneapolis, and an expansion team, also called the Senators, filled the vacancy in the nation's capital.

The expansion Senators were purchased in 1972 by Short and relocated to Arlington, Texas, where they became the Texas

Rangers. Short attempted to capitalize on his relationship with Martin by hiring him away from the Tigers to be his manager.

"Bob," Martin said, "I have a job."

The move from Washington to Texas did little to improve the team, either on the field or at the box office, and when the Tigers fired Martin, Short moved quickly to try once again to bring in the Baseball Doctor.

"I had had two bad experiences as a manager," said Martin, "getting fired in Minnesota and getting fired in Detroit. I didn't want to go through that again. I didn't think I wanted to manage again, but Bob talked to me for four hours, begging me to take the job because it looked like he was going to lose $4 million and he felt I could help him avoid that. When he put it like that, I figured I couldn't say no to him. I owed it to him for all he had done for me. So I took the job."

The change in managers was not immediately hailed in Texas, where Herzog was popular with the fans and respected by the media. In defense of the move, Short said, "I'd fire my mother for the chance to hire Billy Martin."

As a favor to his friend, Martin accepted the same salary he was being paid by the Tigers, even though he had a year to go on his Detroit contract and would have been paid in full by the Tigers while taking the year off to fish, hunt, and play golf. Martin asked for only one stipulation in his Rangers' contract: that he have the last word on personnel. He would make decisions on which players were brought up from the minor leagues and which were sent down, and he would have input on all trades.

Martin used the final 19 games of the 1973 season to observe and acquaint himself with his new players. He would wait until spring training to implement his style and put the Martin stamp on his new team.

Similar to his effect on the Twins and Tigers, the improvement in the Rangers was immediate and miraculous. A team that had won 57 games, finished sixth in the American League West, and drawn 686,085 fans in 1973 won 84 games under Martin in 1974, finished second, and drew 1,193,902 fans. But as he did in Minnesota and Detroit, Martin would soon run afoul of the Rangers' front office.

The logical conclusion is that this was Billy being Billy again, unable to stand prosperity, flexing his muscle, defying authority. Only this time, his insubordination seemed justified. Unable to absorb the financial losses, Short had no choice but to sell his majority interest in 1975 to Brad Corbett.

Corbett, who grew up in the Bronx, had made his fortune by inventing a new type of plastic pipe. He was a baseball novice who thought of himself as an expert, which left Martin yearning for the good old days when club owners such as Colonel Jacob Ruppert, Dan Topping, Del Webb, Phil Wrigley, and Tom Yawkey remained in the background and left the running of their teams to baseball people.

"If Bob Short hadn't sold the club," Martin would say in later years, "I probably would have stayed there for years."

The first sign of trouble came when the Rangers drafted and signed out of high school a left-handed pitcher named David Clyde. Clyde was a local hero who had had a spectacular high school career, and Corbett envisioned him as another Bob Feller, who went from high school to become a Hall of Fame pitcher for the Cleveland Indians in the 1930s.

Martin recognized that while he was talented and had enormous potential, Clyde, who had never pitched on any level above high school, was no Feller. Far from it. Billy urged Corbett to send the kid to the minor leagues, where he could gain experience, learn his craft, and improve.

Corbett, however, insisted on keeping the youngster with the Rangers, figuring that the local high school sensation would put anywhere from 10,000 to 20,000 additional fannies in the seats every time he pitched.

Although he was a curiosity and a local hero and he did, indeed, put people in the seats, as a pitcher, Clyde was a disaster. He made 18 starts in 1973, completed none, and had a 4–8 record and an earned run average of 5.01. He would pitch five seasons in the major leagues with Texas and Cleveland and compile an overall record of 18–33 and an ERA of 4.63.

"What a waste of talent," Martin said. "He could have been a good major league pitcher if he had gone down to the minor leagues like I wanted him to and learned his trade, learned how to pitch. He would have helped the Rangers for years. But they built him into such an attraction that he helped fill the ballpark, and Corbett was shortsighted. He could see only dollar signs and packed houses. He couldn't see beyond today's attendance."

Martin further jeopardized his position when he and the Rangers' traveling secretary, Burt Hawkins, had a disagreement, and Martin slapped Hawkins, a man in his 60s, in the face. Martin and Corbett also clashed on other personnel decisions. The owner wanted to trade for Willie Davis, who had been a big star with the Dodgers in the 1960s and early 1970s, but had been traded to the Montreal Expos after the 1973 season. Martin was against it. He saw Davis as a 35-year-old player who had lost his blazing speed and was over the hill. What's more, Martin didn't like Davis's attitude and was afraid he would be a bad influence on the team's young players.

Corbett won out, and the deal was made. Davis played in 42 games for the Rangers, batted .249, and was traded to the Cardinals in June.

None of this would have necessarily marked the end of Martin's tenure in Texas if Billy hadn't aired the Rangers' dirty linen in public. He complained to the press about Corbett's meddling, and when Corbett read about it, Martin's days in Texas were numbered. He was fired after 95 games, on August 21.

Meanwhile, George Steinbrenner, under suspension from baseball but growing increasingly disenchanted with his own manager, was closely monitoring the situation in Texas. When Martin was fired, Steinbrenner ordered Gabe Paul to contact Billy and offer him the job as manager of the New York Yankees.

Paul tracked Martin to a fishing lodge in Colorado. He reached Billy by telephone and asked him if he would meet with Yankees scout Birdie Tebbetts in Denver. Martin agreed. He checked into a Denver motel and waited for Tebbetts to arrive. Acting as the Yankees agent, Tebbetts made Martin an offer he couldn't refuse, a three-year contract to manage his beloved New York Yankees, albeit one with clauses and codicils with regard to Martin's off-field behavior that would come back to bite him several times.

The deal was completed between Martin and Paul. Steinbrenner never got directly involved in the negotiations, but those who followed the Yankees knew that nothing happened around the team without the owner's knowledge and approval, suspension or not.

As a member of the Indians, Martin had spent the 1959 season in Cleveland, where Steinbrenner was earning a reputation as a bright, young businessman-on-the rise. But during that time their paths never crossed. That was about to change.

Mr. Martin, meet Mr. Steinbrenner.

Four
TWO DIFFERENT WORLDS

They were born two years, one month, 18 days, and some 2,500 miles apart, and yet it's as if Billy Martin and George Steinbrenner came from different worlds: Martin born into poverty, with no strong male role model, the son of a father who abandoned his family when the baby boy was eight months old; Steinbrenner, a child of affluence and privilege, the son of a wealthy but strong-willed, stern, austere, and demanding patriarch.

For all their differences, the two had one thing in common: a fierce and unabated competitive drive, the insatiable desire to succeed. Martin was motivated by a passion to escape his humble beginnings and to prove wrong those who said he was too small and too feeble to make it in professional baseball; Steinbrenner, by a hunger to exceed his father's success and, at the same time, win his sire's approval.

"Winning is the most important thing in my life, after breathing," Steinbrenner once said. "Breathing first, winning next."

Alfred Manuel Martin, Jr., entered the world on May 16, 1928, in Berkeley, California. He was named for his biological father, a musician from Hawaii who was of Portuguese extraction (the name Martin probably derived from an Englishman who migrated to Portugal in the 1400s), but to family and friends, he was "Billy," the name truncated from the Italian word *bellissimo* ("beautiful one"), a term of endearment from his Italian-speaking maternal grandmother.

Martin didn't know his name was Alfred until he was 12 years old. Often he told the tale that on the day he entered junior high school, he waited while a teacher called out the names of the pupils and assigned them to their homeroom class. When the teacher called out the name "Alfred Manuel Martin," there was no response. After all the other students had been assigned to a class, and Martin was the only one remaining, he told the teacher, "You didn't call me."

"What's your name?" she asked.

"Billy Martin."

"What is your address?"

He told her and she said, "Your name is Alfred."

When he went home, Martin told his mother, Joan, of the incident.

"The teacher said my name is Alfred," he said.

"It is," his mother replied.

"Why didn't you ever tell me?" he wondered.

"Because," his mother said, "I didn't want you to know you had the same name as that jackass."

Growing up, Martin never knew his father. It wasn't until Billy was 15 when Alfred Sr. briefly dropped into his life and then quickly disappeared, not to resurface until Billy was playing in the minor leagues and again after he had joined the Yankees.

After Martin's mother threw his father out, she met and later married an Irishman named Jack Downey, a cook on the San Francisco-to-Sausalito ferryboat. Downey was a good man, a hard worker who helped ease the financial burden on the Martin family and who Billy regarded as "my real father."

Because both his mother and stepfather had to work, his grandmother, who lived next door, raised Billy. As a result, the strongest influences in Martin's formative years were female—his grandmother, his mother, and his mother's sister.

Although he kept the Martin name throughout his life, Billy rarely mentioned his Portuguese lineage, but took pride in his Italian heritage. You knew you were in good favor with Martin if he referred to you in one of three ways—as "pard" or "pal" (it was, however, critical to pay heed to his inflection of the word) or "dago" (an affectionate term to Billy that he would bestow upon those he liked regardless of their ethnicity, color, or creed).

Young Martin was obsessed with sports—baseball, football, basketball, volleyball, and boxing. He was proficient in them all, but he was most passionate about baseball. In high school, he read, and wrote a report on, the book *Lou Gehrig: A Quiet Hero,* by Frank Graham. The book made him a Yankees fan. He also was a fan of the Chicago Cubs because Augie Galan, a neighborhood guy (the Martins lived on Seventh and Virginia in Berkeley, the Galans owned a laundry four blocks away on Seventh and San Pablo) was an outfielder for the Cubs and a local hero. The walls of Martin's bedroom were adorned with pictures of Galan and other Cubs sent to him by Augie.

In the summer, Billy would spend most days playing ball until dark in James Kenney Park, two blocks from his home. Soon, he was earning a reputation as a baseball player and a battler.

"My father's fire came from his upbringing," said Billy Martin Jr. "It came from having a mother who was really hard on him. It came from feeling like an outsider in his own family. That can make you paranoid, feeling like an outsider in your own home. He took pride in his energy, his enthusiasm, his strength, his toughness.

"When he was a kid, he'd dare you to call him a 'dago.' If you did, he was coming after you."

On Berkeley High School's baseball team, Martin was the shortstop and cleanup hitter. At the same time, he played for the Junior Oaks, an amateur team sponsored by the Oakland Oaks of the Pacific Coast League. With the Junior Oaks he was befriended by a man named Red Adams, the Oaks trainer, and Eddie Leishman, a minor league manager in Oakland's farm system.

Adams gave Martin money to take the bus from Berkeley to Oakland and for Billy to buy a hamburger and a milk shake after his games.

In his senior year in high school, Martin led his team in batting and was certain the scouts, who often attended Berkeley High games, would come to him with offers to play professional baseball. But none were forthcoming. The word around Berkeley was that the scouts' report on this kid Martin was "too small, too skinny; not a prospect."

Discouraged, Martin spent the summer working at odd jobs and continuing to play ball at James Kenney Park. One day in late July, an Oakland scout named Jimmy Hole contacted him at the suggestion of Eddie Leishman, manager of Oakland's Idaho Falls affiliate in the class D Pioneer League. An Idaho Falls infielder had broken his arm, and Leishman, needing a body for the final six weeks of the season, remembered the tough little infielder from Berkeley and asked Hole to find the kid and send him to Oakland to meet with Oaks owner Brick Laws and another scout, Cookie DeVincenzo.

"Eddie Leishman wants you at Idaho Falls because one of his infielders got hurt," said DeVincenzo. "Do you have a suitcase?"

Martin said he didn't.

"Do you have a suit?"

"I had one," Billy replied, "but they buried my uncle in it."

Laws gave the kid $300, then told him to buy a suitcase and a suit and report to Idaho Falls. He would be paid $200 a month for the remainder of the 1946 season, but there was no guarantee he would have a job in 1947.

Martin didn't even own a baseball glove. He borrowed one from James Kenney Park, which kept a free stash of gloves for the local kids, and off he went to Idaho Falls, where he batted .254 in 32 games, good enough to be invited to spring training the following season, which he spent with Phoenix of the class C Arizona-Texas League. There he led the league in batting with a .392 average, had 230 hits, 48 doubles, 31 stolen bases, and 174 runs batted in in 130 games. The numbers were so spectacular, by season's end, Martin was promoted to Oakland of the class AAA Pacific Coast League, where he came under the tutelage of the man and manager who would have the most profound influence on his baseball life, Casey Stengel.

In 1930, in the Cleveland suburb of Rocky River, Ohio, George M. Steinbrenner III, child of privilege, was born, like song-and-dance man George M. Cohan, on the fourth of July, a real-live nephew of his Uncle Sam.

"I had a typical German father," Steinbrenner said. "He instilled in me discipline and desire. He wanted me to do well in sports, but to also do well in grades. I don't know if I ever measured up to what my dad expected of me, except with the Yankees. He loved the Yankees, and he loved the Indians. He used to take me to see the Yankees when they played in Cleveland. Bill Dickey and Joe DiMaggio were his favorites. After we won the World Series in 1977, my dad said something that got into print: 'Well, he finally made it.'

"My mother was 5 feet, 2 inches tall, and she was Irish. I like to say that's where the best half of me came from. My mother was very important. She kept the family going. If there was any kindness, any of the right qualities in me, which I consider so important, caring for those less fortunate, those qualities came from my mother.

"My dad insisted that none of us get an allowance without earning it. We lived in what was a miniature farm in Bay Village, 11 miles outside Cleveland. We raised vegetables, apples, and chickens. My dad staked me to the chickens. It was my job to raise the chickens and sell the eggs. My dad made me keep the books and learn the value of a dollar when you had to go out and earn it. And that's how I earned my spending money instead of getting an allowance. I knew the chicken business. I was a chicken man."

In the summer of 1947, while 19-year-old Billy Martin was beginning to get noticed as a baseball player, 17-year-old George Steinbrenner was between his junior and senior years at the prestigious Culver Military Academy in Indiana. At Culver, young

Steinbrenner would earn a reputation himself as something of an athlete, a member of the basketball team, an end on the football team, and a track man of considerable promise in his specialty, the low hurdles, an event in which his father had excelled, but one that would soon be eliminated from collegiate track and field.

After graduating from Culver, "Chicken George" was admitted to an even more prestigious institution, Williams College, one of a trio of schools, along with Amherst and Wesleyan, that comprised New England's "Little Three."

At Williams, Steinbrenner dropped the other sports and concentrated on track, setting several school records and being named captain of the Williams track and field team. In his senior year, he went out for football and made the team as a halfback of little distinction.

After graduating from Williams, and with the Korean War winding down, Steinbrenner joined the Air Force, was commissioned a second lieutenant, and assigned to Lockbourne Air Force Base in Columbus, Ohio. He briefly entertained thoughts of making a career out of the military, but the lure of sports was stronger, and when he was discharged from the service, Steinbrenner confronted a dilemma. His father wanted him to join the family business, Kinsman Marine Transit Company, but George was obsessed with pursuing a career in sports. He spent two years as a basketball and football coach at Aquinas High School in Columbus, Ohio, then enrolled at Ohio State University to study for a master's degree in physical education. A year later, he joined the staff of Lou Saban at Northwestern University as ends coach.

When the team lost all nine of its games, Saban was fired, along with his entire staff. Saban returned to college football as coach at Purdue University, and he took Steinbrenner with him as his backfield coach. It was a kindness Steinbrenner never forgot and one he would repay two decades later by naming Saban president of the New York Yankees.

Although he still aspired to a career in coaching, Steinbrenner was growing disillusioned with the uncertainty, nomadic existence, and meager pay of a football coach, especially since he had married and was an expectant father. He gave up his dream of being a coach and acceded to his father's wishes that he join Kinsman Marine as its treasurer.

Five

CASEY'S BOY

Before the Giants and Dodgers moved from New York and Brooklyn to San Francisco and Los Angeles in 1957, the Pacific Coast League was almost a third major league. Players whose careers were winding down—especially those who made their homes on the left coast—found they could scratch out another year or two playing baseball. And the pay, in some cases, was more than they had earned in the big leagues.

In 1948, 19-year-old Billy Martin from nearby Berkeley was assigned to play for the Oakland Oaks of the PCL, a team comprised mostly of former major leaguers:

- Dario Lodigiani, a 32-year-old infielder from San Francisco, had played six seasons with the Philadelphia Athletics and Chicago White Sox.

- Jim Tobin, 36 and an Oakland native, had pitched nine seasons with the Pittsburgh Pirates, Boston Braves, and Detroit Tigers. He won 105 major league games, pitched a no-hitter for the Braves in 1944, and once hit three home runs in a game.

- Ernie Lombardi, 40, also from Oakland, had a 17-year Hall of Fame career with the Brooklyn Dodgers, Cincinnati Reds, Boston Braves, and New York Giants. He had a lifetime batting average of .306 and is the only catcher in baseball history to win two batting championships.

- Harry "Cookie" Lavagetto, 36, another Oaklander, spent 10 seasons with the Pittsburgh Pirates and Brooklyn Dodgers and delivered one of the most memorable hits in World Series history. In Game 4 of the 1947 Series, with his Dodgers trailing the New York Yankees 2–1, Lavagetto came to bat as a pinch hitter with two outs and two runners on against Bill Bevens, who had not allowed a hit. There had never been a no-hit game in the World Series and wouldn't be one until nine years later. Lavagetto drove a shot off the right field fence in Brooklyn's Ebbets Field. Both runners scored to give the Dodgers a 3–2 victory. It was Lavagetto's last hit in the major leagues.

- The manager of the Oaks was Charles Dillon Stengel, known as Casey. He was 58 years old, a former major league player and manager. As a manager, he had been a disaster. In nine years with the Brooklyn Dodgers and Boston Braves, he had one winning season and never finished higher than fifth place. A Boston sports columnist, Dave Egan, nominated as Boston's 1936 Man of the Year a taxi driver whose cab hit Stengel, breaking the manager's leg. Despite his previous failures, Stengel brought to the Oaks a wealth of baseball knowledge, wisdom, and experience, acquired in almost 40 years in the game.

Martin knew he was privileged being surrounded by so much baseball lore. It was as if he were getting a master's degree in the game, and he soaked it all up. He became the kid brother to the veterans on the team. From Lombardi, Martin learned the proper mental approach to hitting. He listened to Tobin and discovered the thought process of a veteran pitcher dueling batters in crucial situations. Lavagetto, assigned by Stengel to be Martin's roommate, helped the kid with the nuances of infield play: positioning hitters on different pitches, gauging the speed of runners, and learning the proper way for a second baseman to turn the double play.

Martin listened carefully when Stengel imparted his managerial philosophy. He soon became a favorite of Stengel, the old man seeing in Martin's hustle, his work ethic, and his competitive fire a carbon copy of himself when Stengel was a young player.

Martin batted .277 for the Oaks in 1948 and helped them win the PCL pennant. He thought he had done enough to warrant a call to the big leagues, especially when Stengel left Oakland to become manager of the Yankees. But the call for Martin didn't come.

Back in Oakland in 1949, Martin's baseball education continued when Stengel was replaced as the Oaks manager by Charlie Dressen, another veteran of the baseball wars with more than 20 years of major league experience as an infielder, coach, and manager. Martin batted .286 in 1949 with 12 home runs and 92 RBI, and the call finally came. His contract and that of outfielder Jackie Jensen, the "Golden Boy," an all-America football star at the University of California, were sold to the Yankees. It was no coincidence that the Yankees purchased Martin's contract soon after Stengel arrived in the Bronx.

Billy Martin, the skinny kid nobody wanted when he graduated from high school, was going to New York; he was going to be a Yankee.

When the brash Martin arrived in the Bombers' St. Petersburg training camp in the spring of 1950, he discovered that his reputation had preceded him. A pitcher named Ralph Buxton, who had played with Billy in the minor leagues, told some Yankee players, "Wait 'til you see this kid Martin. He's a fresh busher."

A week after he was in camp, Martin was sitting at his locker after practice when he heard a voice say, "Hey, dago, you want to go to dinner tonight?"

Martin looked up and couldn't believe he was staring into the face of the great Joe DiMaggio, the team's biggest star.

"Yeah, sure, Joe," Martin gulped. "I'd like that."

Soon it got to be a regular thing. DiMaggio would pass Martin's locker on his way to the shower and say, "Stick around and we'll have a beer."

Before long, they were inseparable: the raw rookie and baseball's greatest player, an unlikely coupling.

One day, Martin heard veteran outfielder Cliff Mapes say, "How come that Martin is going out with the big guy? What does Joe see in him?"

"Yeah," said Johnny Lindell, another outfielder. "Does the punk have something on Joe?"

"You know why Joe is going out with me?" Martin said. "Because he knows class when he sees it, that's why. Joe don't want to hang out with guys with no class."

Early in spring training, coach Frank Crosetti, an outstanding defensive shortstop who had a glorious 17-year major league career as a player, all with the Yankees, had gathered the infielders around him at second base and was demonstrating the proper way to make the double play when he heard a voice say, "That ain't right."

Crosetti looked up to see Martin, hands on his hips, telling the great Crosetti that what he was teaching was wrong.

"Cookie Lavagetto and Charlie Dressen taught me different," Martin said.

Crosetti asked Martin to demonstrate what he had learned. Billy did, and Crosetti admitted Martin's technique was an acceptable alternative. He asked the rookie to teach his method to the other infielders.

With slick-fielding Jerry Coleman solidly entrenched as the regular second baseman, Martin spent his first two seasons with the Yankees as a backup infielder, playing in only 34 games in 1950 and 51 in 1951. By 1952, he had replaced Coleman as the starting second baseman, but after the 1953 season, Martin was drafted into the Army and missed all of the 1954 season and all but 20 games in 1955. By 1956, he had regained his starting position, but little did he know his days as a Yankee were numbered.

In the seven seasons, or parts, that Martin wore a Yankee uniform, the team won six pennants. In 1954, the year he missed because of military service, they finished second to Cleveland.

"He's the kind of guy you'd like to kill if he's playing for the other team," said longtime baseball executive Frank Lane, general manager with the Cleveland Indians and the Chicago White Sox in Martin's era. "But you'd like 10 of him on your side."

Nobody appreciated Martin's unique talent more than his manager and mentor, Casey Stengel, even if the kid was brash and cocky. Billy could get away with behavior under Stengel that others wouldn't even dare try.

Once, when Martin checked Stengel's lineup card taped to the dugout wall and saw that he was batting ninth behind pitcher Don Larsen, Billy was so irate and embarrassed, he pulled the card off the wall, turned it upside down, and taped it back up to make it look like he was leading off. He refused to talk to the old man for days.

Another time, Martin was benched, and once again he showed his anger by giving Stengel the silent treatment. When the game started, Martin took a seat on the end of the bench as far away from Stengel as possible.

In the seventh inning, Martin could see Stengel headed his way. Figuring Stengel was going to tell him to go in on defense, Billy prepared to let his manager have it with all his rancor, until the old man stopped him cold by asking, "Wassa matter? Is widdo Biwwy mad at me? "Will you take your widdo gwove and go out and pway second base?"

Mickey Mantle remembered another time when he and Martin got under their manager's crusty hide.

"If I struck out," Mantle said, "I'd be so pissed off, I'd kick the water cooler or punch it. When Billy struck out, he'd throw his bat or helmet.

"'Look,' Stengel told us one day. 'Strikeouts are part of the game. You're going to strike out. That's OK. I don't want you to throw things or punch things. You might get hurt, or you might hurt one of your teammates. Just laugh it off.'

"That gave Billy an idea.

"'Hey, Mick,' he said. 'Let's try it. The next time you strike out, just laugh it off. And I'll do the same thing.'

"So we did it. I'd strike out, and I'd go back to the bench laughing.

"'Imagine that, ha, ha, ha,' I'd say. 'I struck out again.'

"And Billy would strike out and gently put his bat and his helmet on the ground, and he'd say, 'Ha, ha, ha, how about that guy striking me out with a hanging curveball? Ha, ha, ha.'

"This went on for a couple of days, and we could see that Casey was getting pissed. Finally, one day Billy struck out, and he came back to the bench laughing. The old man looked at him and said, 'All right, that will be enough of that shit.'"

Martin's legacy as a player comes from his performance in the World Series, which established him as a big game player.

"We'd go to the World Series, and the newspapers would always compare the two teams, position by position," Martin once said. "Except for my one pinch-running appearance in 1951, I played in four World Series, and each one was against the Brooklyn Dodgers, in 1952, 1953, 1955, and 1956. I would be compared with Jackie Robinson or Jim Gilliam, and the papers would always give the Dodgers a big edge at second base.

"The photographers would be on the field before the first game of the Series, taking pictures of all our stars—Whitey Ford, Mickey Mantle, Hank Bauer, Gene Woodling, Yogi Berra—and they'd ignore me.

"'Hey,' I'd tell them, 'you'd better take my picture because I'm going to be the star of this thing,' and they would just look at me, laugh and say, 'We don't need you, Billy.'

"'OK,' I'd say. 'Go ahead and leave me out, but you're going to come looking for me to take my picture, and I'm going to be too busy.'"

Robinson was the Dodgers second baseman in 1952. He had batted .308 during the season to Martin's .267, but Robinson hit .174 in the Series with two RBI. Martin batted .217 and drove in four runs.

(Robinson batted .234 in six World Series, 77 points below his regular season career average; Martin batted .333 in four World Series, 76 points above his career average. In 38 World Series games, Robinson had 2 home runs and 12 RBI; in 28 Series games, Martin hit 5 homers and drove in 19 runs. This does not so much discredit Robinson's reputation as a winner, a competitor, and a clutch performer as it affirms Martin's ability to elevate his performance in big games.)

Gilliam had replaced Robinson for the Dodgers and would be their second baseman in the World Series of 1953, '55, and '56. Martin outhit Gilliam in each Series: .500 to .296 in '53; .320 to .292 in '55; .296 to .083 in '56.

Martin's biggest World Series moment came on defense in 1952. It came in the seventh inning of the seventh game with the Yankees leading, 4–2. The Dodgers had loaded the bases with one out, and Stengel replaced pitcher Vic Raschi with journeyman left-hander Bob Kuzava, who got Duke Snider to pop to third baseman Gil McDougald. Robinson then hit a high pop fly to the right side of the infield. Everybody seemed to stop as if in a freeze frame as the ball wafted high atop the second deck in Ebbets Field and, caught in a swirling wind, began drifting back toward the third base line.

Suddenly, while the other infielders remained transfixed, Martin moved. Dashing from his second base position, almost in short right field, he darted toward the third base line as the ball was dropping rapidly and the three runners were racing around the bases. Martin caught up with the ball halfway between the pitcher's mound and the third base foul line, reached over, and snared the ball at his knees just as it was about to drop untouched. His catch saved three runs, the game, and the World Series as Kuzava set the Dodgers down in the eighth and ninth innings and the Yankees won their fourth of an unprecedented five straight World Series.

In 1953, Martin was the offensive star as the Yankees beat the Dodgers for their fifth straight World Series championship. Martin collected 12 hits, a record for a six-game World Series, and led the powerful Yankees of Mantle, Bauer, Woodling, and Berra with a .500 average, two triples, two home runs, and eight RBI.

Martin's contribution to the Yankees' seven-game World Series victory over the Dodgers in 1956 was somewhat subtler, as teammate Bill "Moose" Skowron remembered.

The Yankees, who finally lost a World Series to the Dodgers the previous year, dropped the first two games of the '56 Series but came back to win the next three games, including the only no-hitter in World Series history, Don Larsen's Perfect Game in Game 5.

But the Dodgers won Game 6, 1–0, and the Yankees faced a seventh game in Brooklyn.

"I played the first game of the Series and went 0 for 4, and Casey benched me," Skowron remembered. "I didn't start the next five games. Then we were on the bus going to Brooklyn for the seventh game, and I'm sitting with Billy Martin, and Billy said, 'Moose, you're getting in this game. I'm going to get you in the lineup.'

"I said, 'Are you kidding me?'

"'No,' Billy said. You're in the game today.'

"When we lost the sixth game, Billy was upset, and he went in to see Casey, as only Billy had the nerve to do, and said to Stengel, 'You better put Moose and [Elston] Howard in there. So he got us in the lineup.'"

Hank Bauer corroborated Skowron's story.

"In the sixth game, Jackie Robinson hit a line drive to left field with runners on first and second in the 10th inning," Bauer recalled. "Enos Slaughter took one step in, and the ball went over his head, and we got beat, 1–0. After the game, Billy, who hated the Dodgers with a passion, was in the trainers' room, and he was crying. He went into Stengel's office and closed the door.

"Stengel said, 'What can I do for you, young feller?'

"Billy said, 'You keep playing that National League son of a bitch [Slaughter], and we're going to blow this thing.'

"Casey said, 'Who would you play?'

"And Billy said, 'I'd put Elston Howard in left field, and I'd put Moose back at first.' The next day we looked at the lineup, and there was Moose at first base batting fifth and Howard in left field batting sixth. Billy did it."

Howard, who hadn't been to bat in the first six games, hit a double and a home run. In the seventh inning, Skowron was due to hit with the bases loaded and the Yankees leading, 5–0.

"As Moose came to bat," said Bauer, "Casey whistled at him, and Moose said to [Roy] Campanella, 'Ah, shit, that son of a bitch is going to take me out.' Moose walked to the dugout, and the old man said, 'Take two shots to right and try to stay out of the double play.'

"Moose said, 'OK.'

"The first pitch, Roger Craig threw it low and away, and Moose hit it into the left field seats for a grand slam. Moose came into the dugout, and the old man said, 'That's the way to pull that ball.'"

After the World Series of 1956, Billy Martin was flying high. He was the regular second baseman for a championship team, he was earning enough money to have a measure of financial security for the first time in his life, and, just short of his 29th birthday, he was in the prime years for a professional baseball player.

But his world was about to come crashing down upon him.

Six

THE COPACABANA . . . AND OTHER ARENAS

On the afternoon of May 15, 1957, after a 3–0 defeat of the Kansas City Athletics, the Yankees record stood at 15–8, and they were in second place in the American League, a half game behind the White Sox.

Things were not going as well for Martin. He was batting only .238 with one home run and seven RBI, and he had lost his starting job, at least temporarily, to a rookie named Bobby Richardson, and had not played in the previous three games.

Despite the downward trend of his game, Martin remained upbeat and was looking forward to some relaxation that night with his teammates, a good way to put his slump and his benching out of his mind. His 29th birthday was the following day, and Mickey Mantle and Whitey Ford had organized a birthday party for their buddy. They chose the night of Wednesday, May 15, because the following day was an open date on the team's schedule. An earlier rainout necessitated rescheduling the game for the afternoon of May 16, but arrangements for the party had been made, babysitters had been hired, so the party went on as scheduled.

Comprising the group of 11 were Mantle, Ford, Yogi Berra, Hank Bauer, and pitcher Johnny Kucks with their wives, and Martin, unmarried at the time, who went stag.

The group assembled for dinner at Danny's Hideaway, a popular East Side bistro and a favorite hangout of Martin and Mantle. After dinner, the 11 repaired to the Waldorf-Astoria, where Lena Horne was performing. When the show ended, and it was still the shank of the evening, the wives indicated a desire to go to the famed Copacabana nightclub to see Sammy Davis Jr. perform. A phone call was made, reservations were secured, and off the group went to the Copa.

The party of Yankees and their wives was seated next to a party of 10, 5 members of a bowling team and their wives. The drinks were flowing, obviously taking their effect, the bowlers getting boisterous and making racial remarks about Davis. Bauer, a rugged ex-Marine, told the bowlers to knock it off, and soon words, angry and threatening, were exchanged between Bauer and one bowler who seemed to be the leader of his group.

Bauer nudged Martin. "This guy's giving me a hard time," Bauer said. "There might be trouble. Are you with me?"

Martin said he was, and he followed Bauer outside the ballroom, when another bowler, who was the brother of the loud mouth and who recognized the Yankees, approached Martin.

"Can I talk to you?" he asked Martin.

"Yeah," Billy said, and followed the man into a private room.

"I don't know what's going on between my brother and Bauer," the man said, "but you calm Bauer down, and I'll calm my brother down."

"No problem," Martin said.

At that moment, Martin heard a crash in the coatroom. When he went out to see what happened, "there was the guy who had been bothering Bauer out cold on the floor," said Billy. "Mickey [Mantle] came running over and he was yelling 'Billy, Billy, Billy.' He thought it was me on the floor.

"'Mick,' I said. 'I'm over here.' But some people heard Mickey calling my name, and that's why everybody assumed I had hit the guy, but I didn't hit him. I was nowhere near him."

Because of his reputation, it was understandable that word would spread that Martin was responsible for knocking the bowler flat. Billy, never reticent about professing his fistic ability, steadfastly denied for 30 years that he slugged the guy in the Copa. When Mantle, Ford, and Bauer were asked about the rumble, they all insisted Martin did not hit the guy. The conclusion was that the slugger was either Bauer (he denied it) or a Copacabana bouncer, trying to act as a peacemaker.

The Yankees and Copacabana employees tried to keep the incident quiet, but it leaked out, and the following day it was spread all over the newspapers' front pages.

"When I saw that," Martin said, "I told Mantle, 'I'm gone, Mick.'

"What are you talking about?" Mantle said. "You didn't do anything."

"I know that," Martin said, "but Weiss [Yankees general manager George Weiss] has been trying to get rid of me. He's been looking for an excuse, and now he has it. He's going to blame me, you'll see."

It didn't happen right away. Martin remained a Yankee for another month, but he spent most of the time on the bench and knew his days in pinstripes were coming to an end.

The ax fell on June 15, the trading deadline. The Yankees were in Kansas City.

"Casey didn't like you to sit in the bullpen if you weren't playing," Martin said. "He wanted you to sit in the dugout, but I was so disgusted I couldn't sit in the dugout, and when the game started, I went down to the bullpen so I would be out of sight. I figured if they couldn't see me, they couldn't trade me."

About the seventh inning, Stengel telephoned the bullpen and told Martin to report immediately to the Yankee clubhouse.

"I went to the clubhouse, and a few minutes later, Arnold Johnson, the owner of the Athletics, came in. Casey was talking to me, and he was having trouble getting the words out.

"'Billy,' he said, 'you're going to Kansas City . . . I couldn't . . . Mr. Johnson, let me tell you about this kid . . . '

"You don't have to say nothing," Martin barked at Stengel, cutting the old man off in midsentence. Then turning to Johnson, Martin said, "I'll play for you, Mr. Johnson. I won't dog it on you."

Weiss, who had a keen eye for talent, realized Martin was on the downside of his career and, in young Bobby Richardson, the Yankees had a player who would be their second baseman for many years. Trading Martin and making room for Richardson was sound baseball maneuvering, but Martin, and many others, could not escape the thought that Weiss never liked Martin, his lifestyle, and his fiery temperament. Getting rid of him was not only a way to improve the team's defense and help the Yankees get younger, it was a way to separate Martin from the team's two biggest stars, Mantle and Ford.

"People said I was a bad influence on Mickey and Whitey," Martin would say many years later. "Well, they both made the Hall of Fame, and I didn't. Maybe they were a bad influence on me."

Billy Martin missed New York. He missed the Yankees. He missed Yankee Stadium. He missed his pals, Mickey Mantle and Whitey Ford. He missed playing in the World Series. And he especially missed cashing those World Series checks.

In five years, he bounced around to six different teams, each of them hoping Martin's fire would light a spark, but the spark never came.

Martin was angry. He was frustrated. And he held it against Casey Stengel that he was no longer a Yankee. He believed Stengel could have interceded and prevented him from being traded, but did nothing. A rift developed between the old man and his boy, Billy. They would not reconcile for seven years.

"For many years, Casey was like a father to my dad," said Billy Martin Jr. "And then when Dad was traded from the Yankees, the bane of his existence as a player was that nothing hurt him more, and for a long time he held that against Casey. That aside, what an influence Stengel was. He did take Dad under his wing. Dad always said that was as close to a father figure as he ever had."

"After I was traded," Martin said, "I was so hurt I stopped talking to Stengel because I thought he could have prevented the trade. I'd be playing against the Yankees, and I wouldn't say hello to him or even acknowledge him. If I was at a banquet that he was at, I'd go out of my way to avoid him.

"I know it hurt Casey because he told people, 'The little dago won't talk to me.'

"It was Mickey Mantle who convinced me I was being a baby. He kept telling me, 'Why don't you bury the hatchet? Talk to the old man. He feels bad that you won't talk to him. He's always asking about you.'

"I began thinking about what Mickey said, and I started feeling bad. I thought, 'What the hell are you doing? This man has helped you more than anybody in baseball, and if he dies and you haven't made up with him, you'll never forgive yourself.'"

In 1963, Martin, working as a scout for the Minnesota Twins, attended baseball's winter meeting in Houston. Also attending the meetings was Stengel, manager of the New York Mets. One day, Martin walked into the hotel lobby and saw Casey standing there, holding court, as usual.

"At first, I was going to walk right by him without saying a word," Martin said. "But I decided to say something because I admired him so much. I figured this had gone far enough. I threw my stubbornness and my ego out the window and walked up to him.

"'Hiya, Case,' I said. 'How's everything? How's Edna [Mrs. Stengel]?'

"Casey turned to the writers and said, 'Let me tell you about this guy. This guy was the greatest . . . '

"Like nothing ever happened. After all those years. That's how great Casey Stengel was."

When Stengel passed away in 1975, Martin flew to California for the funeral, stayed in Stengel's home, and, the night before the funeral, slept in Casey's bed.

On June 16, 1957, the day after he was traded to the Athletics, Martin simply moved from the visitor's clubhouse to the home team's clubhouse. It was strange to look across the field and see all his old teammates on the other side. He felt an emptiness in the pit of his stomach.

He had slept hardly at all the night before, having gone out with Mantle and Ford for one last toot. There were tears and drinks; a lot of tears, a lot of drinks.

Martin started at second base and batted second for his new team. It was an odd feeling putting on a Kansas City uniform.

His first time at bat against rookie right-hander Johnny Kucks, who had been one of the Yankees attending Martin's birthday party at the Copacabana, Billy grounded to shortstop. In his second at bat, leading off the bottom of the fourth, Martin hit the ball off the left field wall. Quick fielding by left fielder Yogi Berra held him to a single, but he would come around to score the game's first run.

In the bottom of the eighth, with the Yankees leading 4–3, Martin drilled a home run to tie the score. It was typical Billy, another big hit in a big spot. But there was no joy in him as he rounded the bases, and his home run would turn out to be a wasted effort when the Yankees scored three runs in the top of the 10th to win, 8–5.

Martin's home run against Kucks would be the high point of his season, and his last big hit of the year. Out of Yankee pinstripes, playing for a team that would lose 94 games and finish in seventh place, 38½ games out of first place, was an unfamiliar experience for Martin, and it became apparent that his heart wasn't in it; he was simply going through the motions. He batted .257 in 73 games for the Athletics, and soon after the end of the season, on November 20, he was traded to the Tigers as part of a 12-player deal.

Martin spent one season in Detroit and was traded to Cleveland in 1959. At least he was going to a contending team. The fates, however, were conspiring against Martin. On June 23 in Baltimore, he charged a bunt from his second base position, one-handed the ball, and flipped it to first. As he did, he fell hard to the ground and separated his shoulder. He would miss 19 games.

Back in the lineup less than three weeks later, on September 5 in Washington, Martin and the Indians met the Senators in a doubleheader. Martin had two hits in the first game. Leading off the second game, Martin was hit on the left ear by a pitch from Tex Clevenger. Martin fell to the ground, blood pouring from his nose and his ear. He was removed from the field on a stretcher and taken to a hospital, where x-rays showed Martin had suffered a broken jaw. He would not return to the Indians for the remainder of that season, or any other. On December 15, he was traded for the fourth time in 30 months, this time out of the American League to the Cincinnati Reds.

By then, Martin had completely absolved Clevenger of his beaning. He realized Clevenger did not throw at him intentionally, but at the same time he issued a warning to pitchers everywhere.

"No pitcher is going to throw at me again," he said. "If he does, he's going to pay for it."

On August 4, 1960, the Reds were in Chicago for a game against the Cubs. Martin came to bat in the second inning against a hard-throwing but wild 22-year-old right-hander named Jim Brewer. When Brewer threw a high, tight fastball that just whizzed behind Martin's head, Billy retaliated on the next pitch. He swung and missed and flung his bat toward the pitcher's mound. It landed between the mound and first base.

Martin's defense was that the bat "slipped" and that when he went to retrieve it, Brewer asked him if he wanted to fight.

"No, I'm just out here to get my bat, kid," Martin said.

As Brewer picked up the bat and was handing it to Martin, he took a right hand from Martin that landed flush on the pitcher's right eye, breaking his cheekbone. Martin, whose reputation had preceded him (in addition to his barroom brawls, he had had on-field altercations with Tommy Lasorda, Jimmy Piersall, Matt Batts, and Clint Courtney), received a five-day suspension and a $500 fine from National League president Warren Giles. No penalty was imposed on Brewer, who was hospitalized for two months.

"Nobody, and I mean nobody, is going to throw at my head," Martin said. "They can hit me anyplace else, but not in the head."

The Cubs filed suit against Martin in the amount of $1.125 million for the loss of Brewer's services. Later, the Cubs dropped their suit, but Brewer pursued damages. The case dragged on for years until finally, in 1969, a judge ordered Martin to pay the pitcher $10,000.

"How does he want it?" Martin asked sarcastically. "Cash or check?"

Martin finished out the season in Cincinnati with a .246 average and soon was on the move again. On December 3, 1961, he was sold to the Milwaukee Braves, but after appearing in only six games for Milwaukee, he was traded back to the American League, to the Minnesota Twins, which turned out to be a fortuitous landing place for Martin. He knew his playing career was coming to an end. At age 33, he was going to have to contemplate his future.

While Billy Martin's fortunes were in decline between 1956 and 1960, George Steinbrenner's were on the rise. As treasurer of his father's company, Kinsman Marine, Steinbrenner had found a measure of financial security. But he remained unfulfilled. The seductive lure of a career in sports was still not quelled.

In 1960, Steinbrenner sold his Kinsman stock and headed a group that purchased an AAU Industrial League basketball team, the Cleveland Pipers. One of his first moves as owner of the Pipers was to bring in a new coach, an African American named John McLendon, who had led Tennessee A&I to three consecutive small college national championships in the 1950s.

Steinbrenner's Pipers were a success artistically but not financially, and the Industrial League floundered, its future in serious peril. But as one door was closing for Steinbrenner, another was opening. A new professional basketball league was emerging.

The brainchild of Abe Saperstein, founder and owner of the legendary Harlem Globetrotters, the American Basketball League was designed to rival the established National Basketball Association. Envisioning the new league as an opportunity to jump into the mainstream of professional sports, Steinbrenner pulled his Pipers out of the Industrial League and entered the ABL as a charter member in the 1961–1962 season. As a result, John McLendon became the first black man to coach or manage a team in a major U.S. sports league.

Those paying attention might have looked at the behavior of the owner of the Pipers and seen it as a window into his future machinations as owner of the New York Yankees. He constantly berated his players, coach, and office workers when he was displeased with the team's performance. He screamed at officials from his courtside seat and once was ejected from the arena after a particularly vociferous verbal attack on a referee. And he won the ABL's first championship.

Even then, Steinbrenner spared no expense in accumulating the best available players and management personnel for the Pipers, the best team money could buy. He outbid the NBA's Cincinnati Royals for the services of Ohio State All-American Jerry Lucas, but Saperstein's league folded in December 1962 before Lucas ever could play a game for the Pipers, and Steinbrenner was a rudderless leader. He attempted, unsuccessfully, to obtain a franchise in the NBA.

Having nowhere else to turn, and with his bank account once again depleted, Steinbrenner returned to Kinsman Marine in 1963 as his father was contemplating retirement. Now determined not only to enter the business of his father but also to outdo him, George begged and borrowed enough money to purchase a controlling interest in Kinsman. He also bought 40 percent of the American Shipbuilding Company, combined the two under that name, and, within five years, tripled the revenue of Kinsman Marine. Steinbrenner's success in business got him included on *Cleveland* magazine's list of the top 50 "Movers and Shakers" in the United States. George M. Steinbrenner III was well on his way to becoming a multimillionaire.

But Steinbrenner's lust for sports still raged within him. When he learned in 1972 that his hometown major league baseball team, the Cleveland Indians, was for sale, he put together a group to purchase the team from restaurateur and food mogul Vernon Stouffer. For reasons never made known, Stouffer turned down the offer and sold the team to another group, a severe and disappointing blow to Steinbrenner, a man who by then had become accustomed to getting what he wanted.

His failure to purchase the Indians would turn out to be a blessing in disguise for Steinbrenner. Only a few months after his deal to buy the Indians fell through, he learned from Gabe Paul that the Yankees were for sale. Had he been given a choice between owning the Yankees and owning the Indians, the decision would have been a no-brainer.

When he was introduced as the new owner of the Yankees on January 3, 1973, Steinbrenner said that "the Yankees are the best buy in sports today. I think it's a bargain. Owning the Yankees is like owning the *Mona Lisa*. The Yankees are the greatest name in sports."

And George Steinbrenner was determined to improve the brand and make the name even greater.

Seven

DO YOU TAKE THIS MANAGER?

Old-Timers' Day, an annual rite of summer for the New York Yankees, a day when the past meets the present, has been held for more than 60 years.

Old-Timers' Day has its genesis in Yankee Stadium on July 4, 1939, when, between games of a doubleheader against the Washington Senators, the Yankees staged "Lou Gehrig Appreciation Day" to honor their fallen captain and hero, who had been stricken with a rare and incurable ailment called amyotrophic lateral sclerosis (now known as Lou Gehrig's disease) that attacks the central nervous system. Gehrig would succumb to the ravages of the disease less than two years later on June 2, 1941, just two weeks before his 38th birthday.

Most of his teammates from the famed Murderers' Row Yankees, including the incomparable Babe Ruth, were there on that long ago Independence Day to pay homage to the man who just two months before, on May 2, had taken himself out of the lineup after playing in an unprecedented, and unlikely, 2,130 consecutive games.

Now, his once powerful and indestructible body weakened by his illness, the man they called the "Iron Horse" was at a microphone placed near home plate. In a nervous and halting voice, he fought back emotion as he told his teammates, past and present, and an adoring crowd of 61,808, "Today, I consider myself the luckiest man on the face of the earth."

Not long after his death, Samuel Goldwyn Pictures released a movie of Gehrig's life, *The Pride of the Yankees,* with actor Gary Cooper playing the role of Gehrig. Just as Billy Martin had been fascinated with Gehrig when, in high school, he read the book, *Lou Gehrig: A Quiet Hero,* a young George Steinbrenner, not yet out of his teens, was infatuated with Gehrig after seeing the movie. The film would leave a lasting impression on him. It remains his favorite movie. Many years later, Steinbrenner told author Dick Schaap, "I hate to think how many times I've watched *The Pride of the Yankees* on television. I watch it every time it's on."

For all his many defining qualities, the good and the, er, not so good, Steinbrenner is a sentimentalist and a slave to tradition. It is by his decree (demand?) that the Yankees continue to stage an annual Old-Timers' Day when similar events by all other teams have disappeared because no other team can present the pantheon of stars available to the Yankees.

The team's first official Old-Timers' Day was held in 1946, and it remains an unbroken string to this day, with Steinbrenner instrumental in perpetuating the Yankee tradition. He has been the mastermind behind the installation and upgrading of Monument Park, an area behind the center field fence at Yankee Stadium that is adorned with plaques of the legends of Yankee lore. He has continued the policy of permanently retiring the numbers worn by the greats in Yankee history—Billy Martin's No. 1, Babe Ruth's No. 3, Gehrig's No. 4, Joe DiMaggio's No. 5, Mickey Mantle's No. 7, Yogi Berra's and Bill Dickey's No. 8, Roger Maris's No. 9, Phil Rizzuto's No. 10, Thurman Munson's No. 15, Whitey Ford's No. 16, Don Mattingly's No. 23, Elston Howard's No. 32, Casey Stengel's No. 37, Reggie Jackson's No. 44, and Ron Guidry's No. 49. He named the Tampa spring training home Legends Field and had replicas of the plaques in Monument Park scattered around the grounds of the complex.

With a flair for the theatric, Steinbrenner has used Old-Timers' Day as a vehicle for public announcements certain to titillate the fancy of the team's legion of fans. Such was the case on a steamy, 96-degree Saturday afternoon, August 2, 1975.

The Yankees faced the Cleveland Indians at Shea Stadium in Flushing, their temporary home for two years during the renovation of Yankee Stadium, before a crowd of 43,968 attracted more by the presence of former idols than by the importance of the game. The Yankees began the day with a record of 53–51, in third place in the American League East, 10 games behind the Boston Red Sox.

The night before, after a 5–4 victory over the Indians, Bill Virdon had been informed that he was being replaced as manager of the Yankees.

One by one, the legends were introduced during pregame Old-Timers' Day festivities—*Hank Bauer . . . Moose Skowron . . . Gene Woodling*—the cheers growing in a raucous crescendo with the announcement of each name and the player jogging onto the field to take his place along the first base line—*Phil Rizzuto . . . Whitey Ford*—and then the biggest cheers for the biggest stars—*Mickey Mantle . . . Joe DiMaggio . . . .*

The crowd—bathed in nostalgia, reminiscing about the good old days after having suffered through unaccustomed failure for the past 10 years—was spent. It had been cheering uproariously for several minutes at the parade of past heroes but was unprepared for one more announcement, one more surprise, as the voice of public address announcer Bob Sheppard, "the voice of God," according to Reggie Jackson, bellowed over the loud speakers:

" . . . *and finally, the new manager of the Yankees—Billy Martin . . .*"

And there was Martin in his clean, white Yankee uniform. He appeared out of the first base dugout, trotting out to take his place among his old teammates along the first base line. He reached up to remove his cap and waved it to the adoring crowd, acknowledging the thunderous roar coming from the fans who remembered the World Series catch against the Dodgers in 1952 and the World Series record 12 hits in 1953; who cheered the swashbuckling style with which he played, as well as the battles he waged on their behalf; who remembered the past championships in which he shared and the despair they had known for the past decade; and who saw in the skinny man with the No. 1 on the back of his uniform hope for the future.

Later, Martin would meet with the media and, in a voice choked with emotion, would say, "This is the only job I ever wanted."

Three thousand miles away, in Glendale, California, an old man, feeble and in failing health at age 85, was told by his housekeeper that Billy Martin had been named manager of the Yankees. Casey Stengel, who would die seven weeks later, started to cry.

Billy Martin was unable to work any immediate magic as manager of the Yankees, who would perform no better for him that season than they had for Virdon. They would spurt briefly and close the gap to 8½ games behind the Red Sox, but never get any closer. Under Martin, they would win 30 games and lose 26 and finish in third place, 12 games out of first.

The final two months of the season passed uneventfully for Martin, who spent the time mostly as an observer, making mental notes on which players he wanted to keep and which he wanted to replace. Martin studied what was needed to turn the team around and return it to the customary dominance of his playing days, and he had no doubt he could do it. Of paramount importance to Martin was to rid the team of the slackers and malcontents and to change the culture of the clubhouse and the attitude of the players, who accepted losing matter-of-factly because it had become chronic. Losing was what they knew, what they had experienced, and what they had come to expect.

"Billy basically was demanding," Lou Piniella would say in later years. "He wanted things done right. He demanded of you. Billy was all about winning. He was about toughness. One of the important ingredients in a baseball team is that you have confidence in your manager that he can help you win, and Billy certainly did that."

Martin's silent vow was that things would be different in 1976, when the Yankees, to coincide with the nation's bicentennial celebration, would return to the tradition-steeped comfort of a refurbished Yankee Stadium.

The retooling of the team began almost immediately after the end of the 1975 season. On November 22, the Yankees traded pitcher Pat Dobson, who had won 11 games and lost 14, to Cleveland for Oscar Gamble, a power hitter with the kind of left-handed bat that Martin knew from his experience was a necessary commodity because of the stadium's easily reachable right field fence.

On December 11, at the annual baseball meetings in Hollywood, Florida, general manager Gabe Paul pulled off two trades that would have a major impact, immediate and long range, on the balance of power in the American League.

In the first trade, Paul sent the immensely talented but underachieving Bobby Bonds to the California Angels in exchange for pitcher Ed Figueroa and center fielder Mickey Rivers. Figueroa, a native of Puerto Rico, had won 16 games for the Angels in only his second major league season. Rivers was a speed burner who had led the American League with 70 stolen bases, but who came with a reputation of being indifferent and difficult to handle.

Martin, always supremely confident in his ability to motivate players, scoffed at the negativity of the reports on Rivers and gave his approval of the trade. He wanted the speedy Rivers, "Mick the Quick," to patrol the vast expanse of Yankee Stadium's center field and to serve as his leadoff man and catalyst.

In the second trade, the Yankees dealt George "Doc" Medich to Pittsburgh for three players, rookie second baseman Willie Randolph and pitchers Dock Ellis and Ken Brett.

Medich, an intelligent young man from the Pittsburgh suburb of Aliquippa, Pennsylvania, who was studying to become a doctor, appealed to the Pirates as a potential ace of their pitching staff and as a hometown hero who would be a box office attraction.

Randolph, a native of Brooklyn, New York, was a 21-year-old second baseman who had enormous potential, but whose path in Pittsburgh was blocked by veteran Rennie Stennett.

Ellis had won 93 games in eight seasons for the Pirates, including 19 just four years before, but, like Rivers, he came with baggage, the reputation of a player who was hard to handle. And like Rivers, Martin believed he could prod Ellis into being a big winner once more.

Brett, the older brother of Kansas City's George Brett, was a journeyman left-hander who had bounced around to four teams in eight years, never winning more than 13 games in any season. By mid-May, Brett would be on the move once again, traded to the Chicago White Sox for Carlos May, a veteran left-handed hitter with an eight-year career batting average of close to .300 and a strong positive clubhouse presence.

With the trades, Martin had good reason to be optimistic for the 1976 season. He had improved the team's pitching, power, and defense, Yankee trademarks in their championship years. And with Rivers and Randolph, he had dramatically improved his team's speed, an important element in the style of play that would come to be known as "BillyBall."

It is commonly accepted in baseball that a manager will manage as he played. If he was a pitcher, he will put extra emphasis on pitching. If he was a home run hitter, he will eschew "little ball"—the bunt, the steal, the hit-and-run—and play for the three-run homer. In Martin's case, his style as a player was aggressiveness and daring, sliding hard to break up the double play, taking chances, trying to force opponents into making errors, and he wanted, expected, his players to be a mirror of himself.

"Every single game he managed, Billy was relentless," said Paul Blair, who played for Martin and against him as a member of the Baltimore Orioles, managed by Martin's greatest rival of the '70s, Earl Weaver.

"Billy did everything he could think of to win a ballgame. He made us feel the same way. The most important thing was to win the game for the team. Individual stuff didn't matter. You play 100 percent for the team.

"Strategically, Billy was as good as anybody. The biggest difference [between Martin and Weaver] is that Earl would forgive you if you got into it with him. Billy held a grudge. When you got into Billy's doghouse, you didn't ever get out."

Martin was so upbeat about the makeover of his team, according to his autobiography *Number 1*, he told owner George Steinbrenner: "We're going to win the pennant."

"Win the pennant?" Steinbrenner said with a laugh. "Like hell you will."

"What do you want to bet we'll win it?" Martin said.

"I'll tell you what," said Steinbrenner. "I own some tugboats. If you win the pennant, I'll give you a tugboat."

It wouldn't take long for Martin, with his revamped roster, to make his presence felt. In the second game of the season, against the Brewers in Milwaukee, the Yankees took a 9–6 lead into the bottom of the ninth when Don Money connected for what appeared to be a game-winning grand slam against relief pitcher Dave Pagan. Because of the ear-splitting noise of the Milwaukee crowd, Pagan had failed to hear first baseman Chris Chambliss call a time-out just before Pagan delivered the fateful pitch.

If his pitcher failed to hear Chambliss's call, Martin, who never missed a thing on the playing field, did not. As Money circled the bases, Martin dashed onto the field and protested to the umpires that time had been called and that Pagan's pitch, and Money's home run, should have been nullified. The umpires huddled, and first base umpire Jim McKean agreed that, indeed, Chambliss had called for time before the pitch and McKean had granted it.

The home run was negated, and Money was sent back up to bat. He flied out to right field, and the Yankees held onto their lead for a 9–7 victory. Billy Martin, who thought of everything, had struck again. Yankee fans were delighted. So, too, was their owner.

In the beginning, Billy Martin and George Steinbrenner got along swimmingly.

"Their common denominator," said Martin's lawyer, Judge Eddie Sapir of New Orleans, "was that every day they won a ballgame, the Lord added some life back into each of them. And every day they lost, the Lord took a little life away from them. That was their common denominator: their burning desire to win."

The Yankees won five of their first six games in 1976 and 15 of their first 20. On May 8, they were in first place by three games. By mid-July, their lead was double digits, and the Yankees were off and running to their first American League pennant in 12 years.

For the most part, the season would pass without incident . . . well, almost without incident. In retrospect, there were some small, subtle signs of discontent between Martin and Steinbrenner that, in the years ahead, would bubble over into what would become an ongoing soap opera.

As July drew to a close, the Yankees went into a mild slide. They lost 11 of 15 games, their lead melting from 14½ games to a still commanding 8½, sending Steinbrenner into what would become a familiar panic mode. He told Martin he wanted to go into the clubhouse and talk to the pitchers. Billy was against it, but he agreed to let Steinbrenner have his say.

"He gave the pitchers a rah-rah talk like they were high school kids, not professionals," said Martin, who often accused Steinbrenner of having a football mentality, of not understanding the pitfalls of a 162-game schedule.

"In football, they play once a week," Martin said. "Baseball is played every day, day in, day out. You have to grind it. You're going to hit your bumps in the long season, but you just have to ride them out, and you can't ride them out with pep talks."

"I went in and I got tough," Steinbrenner said. "I told them we're going for something here. You're going to get along, and if you can't get along with your teammate, then just ignore him."

Steinbrenner made his Knute Rockne speech, and Martin stood by silently, shifting embarrassingly from one foot to the other. When it was over, and the owner had left the clubhouse, the pitchers began to mock Steinbrenner and his sophomoric speech.

"They hardly paid attention to anything he said," said Martin.

Said Graig Nettles: "We had a lot of veteran guys, and George would come in and yell at us, or he'd rip us in the newspapers. We knew how to turn him off and put that out of our minds and go out and play the game. And we played well after he'd rip us, and he thought he actually spurred us on to victory. He didn't, but in his mind he thought he did."

Not long after Steinbrenner's clubhouse caper, Martin took another subtle hit. As he walked to home plate to present the lineups to the umpires before a game, he noticed that sitting in the owner's private box was Dick Williams, the man Steinbrenner tried to hire as his manager before settling on Bill Virdon.

Steinbrenner explained to inquiring members of the media that Williams's presence was meaningless and innocent.

"Dick was in town," the owner said. "We're friends and he called me, so I invited him to come to the game. There's nothing to it."

Martin, perhaps somewhat paranoid, read something else into Williams's presence—a form of intimidation by Steinbrenner, an implied threat that Billy had better get the Yankees straightened out because another manager was waiting in the wings, and available.

A five-game winning streak and eight victories in nine games in August reversed the trend and restored the Bombers' lead to 10½ games. They would go on to coast to a wire-to-wire victory in the American League East, finishing 10½ games ahead of Baltimore.

"Billy was a real tactician," said Chris Chambliss, who would have a powerful impact on New York's first pennant in 12 years. "He knew how to get the best out of his players. As far as his off-the-field stuff, you kind of knew that, but we had all kinds of other stuff going on with our club anyway. When it came to between the lines, I thought he was an excellent manager."

The Yankees would beat the Kansas City Royals in the five-game American League Championship Series, clinching the pennant in dramatic fashion on Chambliss's home run in the bottom of the ninth.

As soon as Chambliss's blast disappeared into the right field stands, Yankee Stadium exploded as long-suffering Yankee fans celebrated their team's return to glory. Billy Martin had done it. He had made good on his boast to George Steinbrenner. But his job was not complete.

No sooner had the Yankees clinched their 30th American League pennant—the first in Steinbrenner's regime—the owner let Martin know that he would not be content unless the Yankees won the World Series against the Cincinnati Reds, the vaunted "Big Red Machine" of Johnny Bench, Pete Rose, Joe Morgan, and Tony Perez.

When the Reds blew the Yankees away in four games, Steinbrenner went into a rage. The Yankees had won their first pennant in 12 years and had gone over two million in home attendance for the first time in 26 years, but Steinbrenner was not satisfied.

He stormed into the Yankees clubhouse looking for Martin. He found him in the trainers' room, sobbing hysterically in defeat.

"We won a pennant, but I want a ring," Steinbrenner raged and put his manager on notice that getting swept in the World Series rendered the American League pennant meaningless and was therefore unacceptable. He would settle for nothing less than a World Series championship.

To make matters worse, Martin never received the tugboat he said Steinbrenner had promised him. Steinbrenner's defense was that he had mentioned giving Billy a tugboat as a joke, and that Martin understood it to be in jest. It would not be the first time that Martin and Steinbrenner would draw different conclusions on an issue.

One thing, however, was becoming abundantly clear: The honeymoon between George Steinbrenner and Billy Martin was nearing an end.

Eight
CANDY MAN

Reggie Jackson had first planted the seed two years before. He knew free agency was coming. He had watched his teammate Catfish Hunter gain his freedom and sign a rich free agent contract, and he also wanted out of Oakland, to escape the penny-pinching of owner Charles O. Finley. So, Jackson reasoned, what would be the harm in a little advertising?

With Jackson as their marquee player and the American League's premier power hitter who had led the league in home runs in two of the previous three seasons, the Oakland Athletics had won consecutive World Series championships in 1972, '73, and '74. Having finished seven games ahead of the Kansas City Royals to win their fifth straight American League West division title, the A's were trying to become the first team to win four consecutive World Series since the New York Yankees completed a run of five in a row 22 years before.

To reach their goal, the A's first had to defeat the Boston Red Sox in a five-game American League Championship Series, scheduled to start in Boston's historic Fenway Park on Saturday, October 4.

On the day before the first game of the 1975 ALCS, the two teams worked out in Fenway, first the visiting Athletics, then the home-team Red Sox. With his workout concluded, Jackson, still in uniform, found a seat in the stands down the left field line and watched the Red Sox go through their paces, knowing, no doubt, that a crowd of baseball writers would flock to him like flies to a garbage dump.

Jackson was almost always affable with the press and usually accessible. He considered himself a thinking man's ballplayer, an intelligent man who boasted he had an IQ of 160 ("Out of what?" Mickey Rivers once asked. "A thousand?"), and he liked displaying his extensive vocabulary with these men of words. He would often question the writers about their experiences, about the great players of the past he had not seen but they had, about the game as it was played before he came along. He called most writers by name, and those he did not know, he would ask their names and their affiliation.

Not only was Jackson the key man for the three-time defending world champions, and therefore a prominent player in the upcoming League Championship Series, he was an important news story after making it known that he no longer wanted to play in Oakland for Finley and that he would look to go elsewhere if and when he was able to obtain free agency status.

There were frequent reports that Jackson wanted to play in New York, the cultural and media capital of the world, where endorsements and the opportunity to supplement his player's income would be plentiful; for the Yankees, who had the history and tradition the aware Jackson greatly admired; and for George

Steinbrenner, an owner who had made it clear he was willing, and able, to pay top dollar for talent.

With all this in mind, someone asked Jackson how he felt about one day playing for the Yankees. He paused momentarily and then, staring pointedly at those in the crowd that he knew to be employees of New York newspapers, he replied: "If I played in New York, they'd name a candy bar after me."

It was a revealing comment, supposedly delivered spontaneously, and yet it came across as carefully thought out, studied, and rehearsed for delivery at the propitious moment, and fraught with innuendo. It spoke of Jackson's desire to play in New York. It served notice to Steinbrenner—certain to hear of Reggie's comment—that he wanted to be a Yankee. And it told of Jackson's knowledge of history, for legend had it that the Baby Ruth candy bar was named for the redoubtable Babe Ruth. Reggie was clearly implying that playing in New York, for the Yankees, he would be as big a star as Ruth, big enough to have a candy bar named after him.

It did not matter that the legend was never authenticated; that many believed the Baby Ruth candy bar was named not for Babe Ruth, but for Ruth Cleveland, the daughter of President Grover Cleveland. As far as Reggie Jackson was concerned, he had made his point and introduced his advertising slogan.

"That was typical Reggie," said Matt Merola, Jackson's New York–based agent. "He said it, nobody prompted him. It was not something that we had ever discussed before. It was entirely spontaneous. It was a beautiful line because it said so much in so little."

Although Jackson batted .417 in the ALCS (5 for 12 with 3 RBI and Oakland's only home run), the Red Sox won the series in a three-game sweep and advanced to the World Series against Cincinnati. The final game of the ALCS, a 5–3 Red Sox victory in Oakland, would be Jackson's last game for the Athletics.

As the 1976 season approached, Jackson and Finley were embroiled in a contract dispute. Jackson had filed for arbitration in 1975, asking a salary of $160,000. Finley's counteroffer was $135,000. The arbitrator ruled in favor of the Athletics, but Finley, possibly guilt-ridden, possibly in an effort to ingratiate himself to Jackson, voluntarily gave him a $2,500 raise.

After leading the league in home runs with 36 and driving in 104 runs, Jackson figured he was deserving of a healthy raise for the 1976 season, over his salary of $137,500. Instead, Finley sent him a contract calling for $140,000, which Jackson flatly refused. He countered by proposing to Finley a three-year package totaling $525,000—$150,000 for 1976, $175,000 for 1977, $200,000 for 1978. Not only were the increases nominal for those years and, as things developed in the next few years, would have represented one of the biggest bargains in baseball history, by agreeing to Jackson's proposal, Finley would have been assured of at least three more years of Jackson's services and his potent home run bat.

However, Finley continued to play hardball with his slugger, even with the knowledge that Jackson could refuse to sign a contract and become a free agent after the season. On March 1, Finley exercised his option and, under the reserve clause in force at the time, unilaterally renewed Jackson's contract, adding insult to injury by reducing his salary by the legal limit of 20 percent, down to $112,000. Despite the insult, Jackson had no choice but to go to spring training with the A's.

Six days before the start of the 1976 season, Finley conceded defeat. Realizing he would lose Jackson to free agency after the season and be left with nothing in return, Charlie O. sent Jackson to the Baltimore Orioles in a blockbuster six-player trade.

The Orioles hoped to tie Jackson up long-term, but they foolishly and shortsightedly deemed his asking price of $1.2 million for five years too rich for their blood. Jackson agreed to play the 1976 season for $190,000 and decide his future after the season.

Although he reported late to the Orioles, Jackson had a productive season in Baltimore with 27 home runs and 91 RBI in 134 games, but the Orioles finished in second place in the American League East, 10½ games behind the Yankees.

The Orioles were out of the playoffs, but Jackson wasn't. Recognizing his star status and looking to capitalize on his fame, ABC executives hired him as an expert analyst on their American League Championship Series telecasts between the Yankees and Kansas City Royals.

Jackson watched the Yankees beat the Royals in five games and took particular note of the swashbuckling, daring, exciting style of play the Yankees employed under their fiery manager, Billy Martin.

"There's a manager I could play for," Jackson told millions watching the game on television, a remark that was prophetic but would come back to haunt him.

Free agency came to baseball after the 1976 season, just in time for George Steinbrenner, who was still seething over the Yankees four-game World Series sweep by Cincinnati. Money burned a hole in Steinbrenner's pocket. He couldn't wait to spend it, and free agency would give him the opportunity to put his checkbook where his mouth was and to improve his team in search of the elusive world championship.

The first class of free agents matriculated on November 2, 1976, with 24 players declared eligible, including some of the biggest names in the game. Among them was 25-year-old Don Gullett, a hard-throwing left-hander who was considered one of the best young pitchers in baseball. Not only was he 11–3 for the Reds that season, he was the winning pitcher in Cincinnati's 5–1 victory over the Yankees in Game 1 of the World Series, which made him all the more appealing to Steinbrenner.

Also on the list of free agents was slugger Willie McCovey, outfielder Don Baylor, infielder Bobby Grich, and the heart of Oakland's three world championship teams, reliever Rollie Fingers, catcher Gene Tenace, outfielder Joe Rudi, and Reggie Jackson.

Steinbrenner viewed the merchandise like the proverbial kid with his nose pressed to the window of the neighborhood candy store. And like the kid in the candy store, he wanted it all, but under baseball rules, he could sign only two.

Steinbrenner moved quickly to land Gullett and bolster his pitching staff. But the primary object of his affections was Jackson, over the objections of his manager, Billy Martin, who urged the boss to sign Rudi instead. Martin argued that Rudi was a better all-around player, a skillful defender, an excellent base runner, and a better hitter than Jackson, albeit without as much power.

Steinbrenner disregarded Martin's objections and continued to lust after Jackson, in whom he saw a player with tremendous marquee value to go along with his potent left-handed bat, which made him a better fit in Yankee Stadium with its short right field porch than the right-handed hitting Rudi.

For confirmation of his belief, Steinbrenner sought the opinion of Thurman Munson, the Yankees captain and respected team leader.

"Go get the big man," urged Munson. "He's the only guy in baseball who can carry a club for a month. The hell with what you hear. He hustles every minute on the field."

(Munson may have had an ulterior motive in the Yankees' signing Jackson. He had extracted from Steinbrenner a promise that, as captain, no Yankee would earn more than Munson as long as Thurman was on the team. When Jackson was signed, Steinbrenner hedged on his promise on the grounds that most of Reggie's money was deferred and his annual salary was no more than Munson's. Thurman didn't quite see it that way, and it caused a rift in his relationship with The Boss.)

Munson's endorsement to "go get the big man" was enough for Steinbrenner, who set his sights on Jackson and made an all-out push to sign him. His pursuit was relentless. He is renowned for his impatience and for being an exacting employer, for harassing managers and replacing them at will, for berating employees and firing them for minor lapses.

But there is another side of George Steinbrenner, the side

Jackson saw: charming and gracious, generous and persuasive. In his pursuit of Jackson, Steinbrenner appealed to Reggie's ego. He wined him and dined him and paraded him around New York City, knowing cabdrivers and construction workers would help George in his recruiting.

"Hey, Reggie," they would shout, "are you coming to the Yankees? We love you, Reggie. We need you."

As Steinbrenner figured it would, the attention appealed to Jackson's ample ego.

This was New York, and Steinbrenner sensed Jackson, who was born and raised in a Philadelphia suburb, was educated in Arizona, and earned his fame in Oakland, was really a New York kind of guy. Steinbrenner took him to Fifth Avenue, past all the elegant and expensive shops and the luxurious apartments, and to the famed "21" Club for lunch, and Jackson found this magical tour irresistible.

"He hustled me like a broad," Jackson said. "George can sell sand to the Arabs."

"I remember walking down the streets of New York with Reggie and people recognizing him and coming up to him and asking him if he was going to sign with the Yankees," Steinbrenner said.

"'Come to New York,' they kept saying to him, and I think that had an influence on him. I remember we were walking past the Carlyle Hotel, and Reggie turned to me and said, 'We're embarking on an adventure together.' He certainly was right about that."

"I've always liked George," Jackson said. "He introduced me to people, and he expressed to me that he wanted me there, and he adjusted the dollars. New York had just come off a World Series, and I knew I had a chance to get back there, and that was the focus.

"When I signed, George was nice to me until I didn't play well, and he got on me like he did everyone else."

While Jackson was getting the full-court press from Steinbrenner, Billy Martin was steaming. He read in the newspapers about the pursuit of Jackson, about lunch at "21," and he felt betrayed.

"George was taking Reggie to the '21' Club for lunch all the time," he said, "and I was sitting across the river in my hotel room in New Jersey all winter and George didn't even take me to lunch once."

The coronation was held at a gala press conference in the Americana Hotel to announce that the Yankees had signed Jackson, about whom his former Oakland teammate Darold Knowles had once proclaimed, "There isn't enough mustard in the world to cover that hot dog."

Thurman Munson attended the press conference, giving tacit approval to Jackson's arrival. So did veteran Yankee Roy White. Conspicuous by his absence was Billy Martin.

Perhaps it was just as well that Martin boycotted the gala event. Martin might have choked on the ice cube in his drink if he had heard Jackson say he didn't come to New York to be a star, he brought his star with him.

Word trickled out that Jackson's deal with the Yankees would pay him $3 million over five years, almost three times as much as he asked from the Baltimore Orioles. At the time, the expenditure by the Yankees was viewed as a king's ransom, but in retrospect, it would prove to be a bargain, and the best of all the free agent signings.

It also would be the start of some spectacular fireworks involving the team's owner, manager, and star player.

Nine

THE LAST STRAW

If he was nothing else, Billy Martin was stubborn, a quality that for him was both a blessing and a curse.

The blessing was that he possessed the courage of his convictions. Once he formed a positive opinion about a player, he was unbending in that opinion, even when others disagreed. If he believed in a player, he was patient through the difficult times, and he would give that player every chance to succeed. He did it with Rod Carew and César Tovar in Minnesota, with Willie Horton, Joe Coleman, and Ron LeFlore in Detroit, with Mike Hargrove and Jim Sundberg in Texas, with Willie Randolph and Ron Guidry in New York, and with Rickey Henderson and Dwayne Murphy in Oakland.

Billy Martin's curse also was that he possessed the courage of his convictions. Once he formed a negative opinion about a player, he was unbending in that opinion. He did it with Reggie Jackson.

From the start, Martin argued against signing Jackson. He didn't like what he perceived to be Reggie's me-first attitude, his braggadocio, his swagger, his ego. He didn't like Jackson as a ballplayer, and he begged George Steinbrenner to sign Reggie's Oakland teammate Joe Rudi as a free agent instead of Jackson. Steinbrenner wanted Jackson, Martin didn't.

George Steinbrenner was right.

Billy Martin was wrong. He was dead wrong.

"I remember being in Yankee Stadium, in the clubhouse," said Fran Healy, a backup catcher to Thurman Munson with the Yankees in 1977. "It was in the winter, and I was in the sauna. It was just me and Billy. Jackson had just signed, and I didn't know Reggie except as an opposing player, and Billy said to me, 'I'll show him who's boss.'"

Martin often boasted that he didn't believe in playing favorites, that he treated all of his players alike. And yet there are successful managers who have admitted to a double standard in dealing with players. Sparky Anderson was one.

"When you do for me what Johnny Bench, Joe Morgan, Pete Rose, and Tony Perez have done," he often said, "then you will get special treatment, too."

Martin arrived in Fort Lauderdale for spring training, 1977, with the first wave of Yankees pitchers and catchers, on February 24. Five days later, the nonpitchers and catchers reported, Jackson included. Writers covering the team flocked to Jackson's locker and waited to see how Martin would greet his new player. They waited in vain.

It was Martin being Martin, and it was a big mistake. Had he left his office the moment Jackson arrived, gone to Reggie and welcomed him, flattered him with a hearty handshake and a pat on the back, things might have been different. Martin might have saved himself a great deal of future unpleasantness.

Jackson was not entirely blameless, however. His performance at the press conference announcing his signing with the Yankees was tinged with arrogance and bravado.

"I came to New York and said some things," Jackson said. "One of the questions was 'What do you think about becoming a star in New York?' And I said, 'I'm not coming to New York to become a star, I'm bringing my star there.' A lot of people thought that was a bragging, outspoken, egotistical statement. 'Hey, man, what's the matter with you? I've already been in three World Series. I won a Most Valuable Player award in the Series and in the season. What do you mean I'm going to become a star in New York? I'm not coming to become one. I already am.'

"There was a time when as a black man, you didn't speak, you didn't ruffle feathers. You were supposed to be glad just to be in the big leagues, to be in the white league, and to have the opportunity. But I felt I belonged just as much as the next person if I could perform on a certain level. I was looked upon as controversial, a loud mouth, a problem, where the white player was looked on as intelligent."

Jackson dearly wanted to be accepted, to be loved, to be appreciated, and Martin, stubborn to a fault, his fatal flaw, failed on that first day of spring training by refusing to humble himself and welcoming him. His rationale was that he was determined to treat all players, the subs and the stars, equally.

Martin's reaction to Jackson's arrival was to practically ignore him, a cold war from day 1 that created a barrier between manager and player. Jackson's new teammates were only slightly less hostile. They seemed to speak to him only when he spoke to them first, causing Jackson to feel ostracized, an island in a sea of indifference.

To exacerbate the situation, Martin told the writers that he planned to bat Jackson fifth or sixth in his batting order. Another mistake. Give the big man his due, stroke his ego, and Martin could easily have won Jackson over and gotten his loyalty and his respect. Jackson was ready to go through walls for Martin if only Billy had given him the chance.

"Billy did everything he could not to hit me cleanup," Jackson said.

Batting fourth, or third, was a source of pride for Jackson, a validation of his ability and his importance to a team.

"For a guy like Reggie," said Fran Healy, "a guy like Mickey Mantle, a guy like Willie Mays, guys that feel they should be batting third or fourth, I can understand why they would be bent out of shape."

One of the rites of spring training is that star players and veterans often get days off and rarely are asked to make long, tedious, and debilitating bus trips. But it soon became obvious that Jackson was playing every game, making every trip. I asked Reggie about it.

"Oh, you've noticed that, have you? Don't ask me," Jackson said with a nod toward the manager's office. "I don't know what he's trying to prove."

When I told Martin what Jackson had said, Billy was stunned.

"He said that?" Martin shrieked. "He asked to play. He told me he likes to play a lot of innings in spring training."

While his cold war with Jackson simmered, Martin had other problems that spring. The Yankees were losing as many games as they won, and the owner was getting restless. He also was embarrassed.

Steinbrenner had scheduled the Yankees to play a game against the University of Florida on March 23, a night game under lights donated by the boss of the Yankees, who was not pleased by a mere

10–9 victory over a college team. As if that weren't enough to set off an explosion from Mount Steinbrenner, three nights later, the Yankees were beaten by the Mets, 6–0, in a game televised back to New York from St. Petersburg, right near Steinbrenner's Tampa home and in front of many of his friends and neighbors. George hated losing to the Yankees' city rivals any time, even a spring training game, and he hated it even more if the game was televised.

Steinbrenner was already feuding with Martin, who refused to stay in the team's hotel headquarters and chose instead to room with his buddy, Mickey Mantle, about 15 miles north of Fort Lauderdale in Boca Raton. Steinbrenner also wanted his manager to ride the team bus with his players, but Billy preferred to drive his own car to games. When he saw Martin's car in the parking lot after the loss to the Mets, Steinbrenner charged into the Yankee clubhouse and sought out Martin.

"I want to see you now," Steinbrenner boomed angrily. "I want you to ride the team bus."

"George," Martin argued, "I like to ride with my coaches so we can talk about the team."

"You lied to me," Steinbrenner persisted. "You told me you would ride the bus."

"You don't tell me where to ride," Martin replied, his voice rising to match Steinbrenner's anger.

"I ought to get rid of you right now," said Steinbrenner, delivering the ultimate threat.

"Why don't you fire me right now?" Martin exploded, slamming his fist against an ice bucket and splattering cubes onto Steinbrenner and Gabe Paul.

The next morning, Paul brought Steinbrenner and Martin together over breakfast in the Tampa hotel owned by Steinbrenner.

The Boss said his mea culpa over invading the clubhouse and confronting his manager in front of the players and the press, and an uneasy truce settled over the Yankees camp for the final two weeks of spring training. The truce would be short-lived.

The Yankees started the season sputtering. They lost 8 of their first 10 games, and nerves were slightly frayed. A series of minor skirmishes gave a hint to the kind of season it was going to be.

Sparky Lyle and Ed Figueroa were each fined $100 for sleeping through one of Steinbrenner's clubhouse pep talks. Lyle and Mickey Rivers were each fined $500 for missing an exhibition game in Syracuse. Graig Nettles, who had walked out of training camp because he was unhappy with his contract, refused to attend the team's "Welcome Home" dinner.

"If they want someone to hit home runs, they have me," Nettles said. "If they want somebody to attend banquets, they can get Georgie Jessel."

The fast start as a Yankee that Reggie Jackson was hoping for never materialized. After 10 games he was batting .194 with one home run and one RBI, an early $3.5 million bust. He had batted in the third position twice, fifth four times, sixth twice, and twice Martin, miffed because Jackson had told the writers he had a sore elbow, benched him, even refusing to use him as a pinch hitter in extra innings.

On April 20, as the Yankees prepared to face the Blue Jays in Yankee Stadium, Jackson was hitless in his last 10 at bats, one for his last 16. To shake things up, Martin decided to use an old ploy. He told the writers that he had placed the names of his nine hitters in a hat and claimed he made out his lineup in the order in which the names were selected. Martin used the occasion to extend an olive branch to his slumping slugger and gave

Reggie Jackson the honor of selecting the names out of the hat. The random lineup had Willie Randolph batting first, Thurman Munson second, Jackson third, and Graig Nettles fourth, leading to the suspicion that Martin had written down some names on his lineup card before the draw.

The ploy worked. The Yankees erupted for a 7–5 win. Randolph had three hits, including a home run. Munson had two hits and an RBI. And Jackson snapped out of his batting funk with two singles and two runs batted in.

That released the growing tension around the Yankees, who ran off six straight wins, lost one, won five in a row, lost another, and then won three straight. With 14 wins in 16 games, the Yankees moved into first place on May 8, a half game ahead of the Orioles, as they embarked on a West Coast trip to Seattle, Anaheim, and Oakland.

The Yankees had turned things around, as Martin knew they would, but in the world of Billy Martin–George Steinbrenner–Reggie Jackson, trouble was never too far away.

Martin had been asking the Yankees to bring back catcher Elrod Hendricks, a veteran left-handed hitter who had been sent to Syracuse in the International League. Martin believed the Yankees needed another lefty bat off the bench and another catcher. He reasoned that when a team has only two catchers, the manager cannot use the second one because he has to hold him back in the event the No. 1 catcher is injured. As a result, Martin found himself managing shorthanded.

Martin mentioned this to Gabe Paul, and the Yankees president suggested he come to Paul's office before the team went west to discuss the situation. Martin, with his gift for self-destruction, never showed up for the meeting, a violation of a clause in his contract.

When the Yankees lost the first game of their seven-game trip, a 5–2 defeat by the Mariners, Martin, in violation of another clause in his contract, complained to the writers that he was being forced to go to battle with a shorthanded roster.

"I've been asking for Elrod Hendricks for a week and a half," Martin said. "Why are we going with 24 players? It cost us tonight's game as far as I'm concerned."

When Steinbrenner read Martin's comments, he hit the roof. He discussed with Paul the possibility of firing Martin on the spot, but reconsidered and would reach what would become a common compromise. He ordered his public relations department to release a statement that the Yankees were honoring Martin's request to add a player from their Syracuse farm team, but that the extra player would be Dell Alston, who was batting .338, not Hendricks, the catcher Martin wanted, who was batting only .105.

What was not included in the statement was the fact that for his insubordination and violation of the clause in his contract, Martin was being fined $2,500.

Martin had dodged a bullet. The Yankees completed the West Coast trip with a record of 3–4, and on May 19 they returned home still in first place and right into the middle of a hornet's nest.

As they prepared to begin a four-game series against the second-place Orioles, the Yankees were buzzing with word that being circulated were advance copies of an upcoming *Sport* magazine article containing some inflammatory and disquieting statements from Reggie Jackson. During spring training, Jackson had sat down in a Fort Lauderdale pub with a writer named Robert Ward and unburdened himself.

"This team, it all flows from me," Ward quoted Jackson as saying. "I've got to keep it going. I'm the straw that stirs the drink.

It all comes back to me. Maybe I should say me and Munson. But really he doesn't enter into it. He's so damned insecure. Munson thinks he can be the straw that stirs the drink, but he can only stir it bad."

Jackson's defense was that he was misquoted.

"For four pages?" Munson asked.

The article was a torpedo in the turbulent sea that was the Yankee clubhouse. Munson was stung by Jackson's words. His teammates, who respected their captain and viewed him as the heart and soul of the team, rallied around him. His manager sided with him. Jackson, whose relations with his new teammates and his manager were already strained, became more of an outcast. Stung by Jackson's words, Munson would not shake Reggie's hand after a home run.

"The Roger [sic] Ward article in *Sport* magazine, came out and that made things worse," Jackson declared. "If there were any doubts about whether I was a good guy or not, that made it bad because I had seemingly attacked the love of the Yankees, who was Thurman Munson. I didn't mean to, but it was a social quirk, it was a mistake, it was the wrong use of words. I brought that on myself. And anyone on the fence, whether it was Billy or not, it turned them against me.

"In the article, I said something that was misinterpreted by . . . Ward, that 'I'm the straw that stirs the drink; Thurman can only stir it bad.' *That* I never said. Here was a team that had just been beaten by Cincinnati four straight [in the 1976 World Series]. They need one more thumper. They need one more guy. I'm the final ingredient. They've got everything there in the mix. They need one more thing. The guy said to me, 'So you're like the stirrer. You're the final thing. You're the guy that stirs all that.'

"'Yeah, sounds good.' I never made the comment, but that was . . . Ward's deal, so what was I going to say? He put quotes around it and bang!"

After a cooling-off period of a few weeks, Munson's wounds began to heal, and tensions eased. Jackson's bat began to warm, and he tried to thaw the cold war with Munson by offering little peacemaking overtures, a nod, a kind word, praise for Munson to the press that Reggie knew would be printed and, he hoped, read by the catcher. In mid-June, Reggie had a 14-game hitting streak, and Munson, ever the team player and taking his title of captain seriously, began to shake Jackson's hand after a home run.

Despite the relative calm between Jackson and Munson, controversy still remained the order of the day around the Yankees.

Someone referred to the Yankees as the "Bronx Zoo," a name that caught on and stuck, prompting third baseman Graig Nettles, with his acerbic wit, to crack, "When I was a kid, I wanted to do two things: play major league baseball and be in the circus. I'm lucky. I got to do both."

Distractions came almost daily. George and Billy. George and Reggie. Reggie and Billy. But they were not alone. It seemed to be an epidemic, a daily soap opera that spread throughout the entire team like a brush fire out of control. When one flame was doused, another erupted.

The biggest eruption would come on a Saturday afternoon in Boston.

Ten

DUEL IN THE DUGOUT

Full-scale war broke out for the Yankees in the visitors' dugout in Boston's Fenway Park on Saturday afternoon, June 18, 1977. All the tension, all the turmoil, all the frustration, all the festering hostility that had been building for months erupted in an ugly scene in full view of 34,603 fans and a national television audience, including Yankees owner George Steinbrenner, watching from his home in Tampa.

"Reggie Jackson and Billy Martin were opposite people," said relief pitcher Rich "Goose" Gossage. "Billy was always looking for a fight, and Reggie usually gave him a reason."

It came in the midst of what would be a three-game sweep by the Red Sox, which would leave the Yankees two and a half games behind the Red Sox and add to the frustration and rising tempers. Jackson was slow retrieving a ball hit into right field by Jim Rice, who raced around first base and chugged into second.

"The ball was hit over [Willie Randolph's] head," remembered first baseman Chris Chambliss, "and Billy didn't like the way Reggie went after it."

Jackson said it was caution. Martin said it was indifference.

Martin called a time-out and headed to the mound to make a pitching change. Jackson took advantage of the respite to wander over to the Yankees bullpen, unaware that Paul Blair was headed out to right field, having been sent there by Martin to replace Jackson.

"I was in the bullpen, and Reggie was leaning over the railing," recalled Fran Healy, a backup catcher with the Yankees. "I thought Reggie had lost his confidence in the outfield at the time. You knew he didn't want the ball hit to him. Rice's ball fell in front of him, and he really had no shot at catching it. Then he was talking to me, and I saw Blair running out, and I said, 'Uh, oh, I think Billy wants you.'"

When he saw Blair, Jackson was perplexed, astonished, and embarrassed.

"You here for me?" Jackson asked.

Blair nodded.

"What the hell's going on?" Reggie asked.

"You've got to ask Billy that," Blair said.

Jackson trotted in from right field to the Yankee dugout and ducked into the far corner, on the opposite side to where Martin stood, fuming. As Jackson arrived in the dugout, Martin left his place and headed toward the end of the dugout where Jackson was. Jackson had removed his eyeglasses and carefully placed them on the dugout bench as if anticipating a physical confrontation. There were words, and then Martin, red-faced, veins bulging in his neck, was attempting to get at Jackson and being restrained in a bear hug by coach Yogi Berra.

This was Martin's version of the incident:

"I didn't like the way Reggie went after the ball. I thought he dogged it, and I just can't have that sort of thing on my team. I had told my players at the beginning of the season if they embarrassed me on the field, I was going to embarrass them. I knew the other 24 players were looking to see how I was going to handle this, with Reggie being a superstar and having the big contract. I thought if I did what had to be done, that would bring George down on me. But if I let it pass, I would lose the other 24 players.

"I knew what I had to do. I told Paul Blair to go out to right field and tell Reggie he was being replaced. I meant to teach him a lesson.

"When he came into the dugout, Reggie challenged me. He kept telling me he didn't like being shown up, and I replied, 'If you show me up, I'll show you up.' Then he swore at me, and that did it, we almost came to blows. Elston Howard and Yogi Berra had to pull us apart."

This was Jackson's version:

"I'm sure Billy thought I didn't hustle after the ball. He was wrong. Hustle had nothing to do with it. It wasn't the greatest play I ever made in the outfield, but I was giving it 100 percent, even if it didn't look that way to Billy.

"Billy accused me of loafing, and he never changed his opinion, his thought, his expression, so certainly that's imprinted in people's minds that he said I loafed on the ball, didn't try, and that's not what I'm about.

"When he sent in Paul Blair to take me out of the ballgame, it never entered my mind that he was showing me up. When I got to the top step of the dugout, I could see there was a fury about Billy, and it was directed at me.

"'What the bleep do you think you're doing out there?' he screamed at me.

"'What do you mean?' I said. 'What are you talking about?'

"He started down the dugout toward me. 'You know what the bleep I'm talking about. You want to show me up by loafing on me? Fine. Then I'm going to show you up. Anyone who doesn't hustle, doesn't play for me.'

"'I wasn't loafing, Billy,' I said. 'But I'm sure that doesn't matter to you. Nothing I could ever do would please you. You never wanted me on this team in the first place. You don't want me now. Why don't you just admit it?'

"The next words I heard were, 'I ought to kick your ass.'

"And then I'd had enough. I snapped. 'Who do you think you're talking to, old man?' I said.

"'What?' Billy yelled. 'Who are you calling an old man?'

"He came for me. Elston Howard and Yogi grabbed him. Jimmy Wynn grabbed me from behind. I was livid, but I wasn't going to fight him in the dugout. I walked past everybody into the tunnel and headed for the clubhouse. I could still hear Billy screaming from behind me. I was going to wait until the game was over because I lockered right close to the door, and I was going to challenge him when he came in.

"Fran Healy came into the clubhouse and told me to get dressed and get out of the clubhouse, go home because he felt there was going to be an explosive situation. You can't fight the manager. You can't get in a fistfight with him; you'll be blackballed from baseball.

"I wasn't Billy's choice as a player in the free agent draft, but George picked me because Munson told him to. And that's what George did. He didn't pay any attention to what Billy thought, and Billy always thought it was his team. One of the reasons he didn't want Reggie was that they needed a shortstop, and he was heavily laden with left-handed hitting.

"I don't think Billy Martin had a dislike for me. He didn't know me. Billy was not part of that decision, and that's what grinded him. I'm sure he tried to get under my skin, and he did to a point, but I held together."

Billy Martin Jr. could see both sides of the rift between his father and Jackson.

"I think the problems with Reggie were on account of Dad felt like Reggie didn't hustle all the time. When I look at Reggie and I look at his game and the things he did, I don't believe it was that he didn't hustle. Look at the way Reggie ran bases: going hard into second base to break up a double play, always trying to put his body between the baseball and the base he was running to. That's not what a guy who doesn't hustle does. That's not what a guy who doesn't care about winning does. In the outfield, Reggie didn't want to be the guy on *SportsCenter* with the ball bouncing off his head and over the fence. I think it was more that issue than a lack of hustle.

"I know there was a respect there, maybe not a love or a friendship. The big argument in the dugout, I still maintain that Reggie wasn't dogging it. He just didn't want to look bad.

"If you watch the video of that incident, and you see guys being held, you see Reggie say something that sets my father off. He goes berserk there. That's when he's really trying to get at him. What Reggie said there was, 'Hey, you embarrassed me in front of 50 million people. What do you think you're doing, old man?' Dad heard 'old man,' and that was it, he just snapped. He probably never heard that before. It didn't sit too well." (At the time, Martin was only 49 years old.)

Later that night, Steve Jacobson of *Newsday* and Paul Montgomery of the *New York Times* and I went to Jackson's room. Mike Torrez, the Yankees starting pitcher that afternoon, was there to console his friend. Jackson appeared to be near a breakdown. First he was calm, and then he grew increasingly passionate and self-absorbed, talking about "the magnitude of me." He was stripped to the waist, medals and chains around his neck. Perspiration glistened on his bare chest, and soon tears were streaming down his face.

He was on his knees, as if in prayer, delivering a sermon that made him seem like an evangelist, pouring out his anger, frustration, and anguish, wondering why he was being persecuted, why he was so misunderstood, unappreciated, and unwanted. The sweat and tears formed a small pool on the floor at his knees.

"It makes me cry the way they treat me on this team," he wailed. "I'm a big black man with an IQ of 160, making $700,000 a year, and they treat me like dirt. They never had anyone like me on their team before."

Sitting at home, watching the game and the dugout scuffle on television, George Steinbrenner was appalled. His first impulse was to fire Martin on the spot, but Gabe Paul intervened. He told Steinbrenner that to do so would be taking sides with Jackson, and it would appear that Reggie was running the team. Paul offered to bring Jackson and Martin together the next day for a form of baseball détente. Steinbrenner accepted Paul's suggestion and backed off, while Martin met with Jackson under supervision by Paul. Player and manager would reach an accord, although years later Jackson would say, "I forgive, but I can't forget it."

The combination of George Steinbrenner, Billy Martin, and Reggie Jackson was a strange and unholy alliance.

"It was Reggie versus Billy, Billy versus me," said Steinbrenner. "Reggie said this and Billy said this, and there was a triangle there."

It seemed that at the apex of the triangle was control—Steinbrenner controlling Billy, Billy controlling Reggie, Reggie controlling the media. The pot was boiling constantly, and it wasn't always George, Billy, and Reggie. Almost every Yankee got his 15 minutes of notoriety. In Steinbrenner's world that meant headlines and attention, but not apathy, never apathy. Steinbrenner didn't see that as a bad thing.

The 1977 Yankees were made up, in Steinbrenner's words, of "a bunch of personalities that didn't always mix. But you have to have a little bit of turmoil. I'm one that believes a ship gets nowhere in a calm sea."

A few days after the Fenway fracas, Steinbrenner called a press conference at which he outlined those things by which a manager should be judged. They would come to be known as "George's Seven Commandments."

1. Does he win?
2. Does he work hard enough?
3. Is he emotionally equipped to lead men?
4. Is he organized?
5. Does he understand human nature?
6. Is he prepared for each game?
7. Is he honorable?

The writers attending the press conference joked that Martin passed Steinbrenner's test, 4–3.

The incident in the dugout behind them, the Yankees began to play more consistently and in relative peace, until early August, when Thurman Munson, who still had not put Jackson's *Sport* magazine remarks completely behind him, openly defied George Steinbrenner's rule against facial hair by growing a beard. Earlier in the season, Munson had asked to be traded to Cleveland so he could play close to his home in Canton, Ohio. His request fell on deaf ears, and the writers wondered if with the beard, the captain was making a statement, trying to prompt a confrontation with Steinbrenner. Was he asking for a fight with Steinbrenner?

"I'm not asking for anything," Munson replied. "I like beards. Some of you guys [the writers] have beards. They look good."

But, Munson was told, by keeping his beard, he was defying a team rule.

"Isn't that against the Constitution?" he wondered. "Isn't that against the employment act or something? I'm worried about my hitting, not my beard. Did you notice how short my hair is? Some guys have long hair. I got a haircut yesterday. I'm trying to keep up with the team code—short hair, team man, team player. Billy doesn't mind the beard. If Billy doesn't mind, that probably means George does mind."

"We have a code, and I hope he follows it," Martin said. "I'd like to see him cut it off. I'm going to ask him as a friend. I can't force him, he's too hard a player for me to try and force him. If that's a reflection on me, that's a reflection on me."

A few days later, Martin, seeking to avoid another confrontation with Steinbrenner, appealed to Munson to shave his beard.

"Do it for me," Martin pleaded. "As a friend."

Munson shaved, and soon peace, at least temporarily, came to the Yankees. On August 10, Martin swallowed his pride, abandoned his stubbornness, and installed Jackson in the cleanup spot, where he would remain for the rest of the season, hitting 13 home runs and driving in 49 runs in the final 53 games.

On September 25 in Toronto, the Yankees swept a pair of games from the Blue Jays on shutouts by Ed Figueroa and a skinny left-hander named Ron Guidry, who won his eighth straight decision for his 16th win.

Prior to the 1977 season, Guidry had not won a major league game and, in fact, was ready to quit baseball until his wife, Bonnie, talked him out of it. In the spring of 1977, after being battered by the Tigers in an exhibition game in Lakeland, Guidry came frighteningly close to being traded to the Chicago White Sox. The deal was set, but the Yankees reneged at the last minute.

What, and who, caused the Yankees to reconsider is open to interpretation.

George Steinbrenner: "Gabe [Paul] and Billy [Martin] wanted to make the deal, but I talked them out of it."

Gabe Paul: "George and Billy wanted him out of here, but I told them over my dead body."

Billy Martin: "George and Gabe were all set to trade him, but I argued against it."

Riding the pitching of Guidry, Figueroa, and Mike Torrez, and Jackson's potent bat, the Yankees won 40 of their last 53 games and won their second consecutive American League East championship.

"Once we got on a roll," Chris Chambliss said, "we had so many tools, so many weapons to win ballgames that we were going to be able to come out of any slump because we had pitching, speed, and power. When it was between the lines, we all had one task, and we knew what that task was. We knew how to do it, and we had all these weapons to get it done. I feel that's more important than anything. You can be dysfunctional in the clubhouse and still win on the field."

The Yankees had come through the turbulent waters, and for the second straight year, they would face the Kansas City Royals in the American League Championship Series. The long, hard struggle of the regular season was behind them. The turbulence was not.

Eleven

MR. OCTOBER

The American League Championship Series rematch between the Yankees and Royals was just as intense as the first time around the previous year. Once again, they split the first four games, and it all came down to a sudden-death fifth game, this time in KC's Kauffman Stadium. And it would not come without yet another controversy.

When Reggie Jackson arrived at the ballpark, he noticed that his name was not in Martin's starting lineup. With left-hander Paul Splittorff scheduled to pitch for the Royals, and with the game to be played on fast artificial turf and the Royals lineup stacked with speedsters, Martin decided to replace Reggie in right field with Paul Blair, a far superior defender than Jackson. It was a more subtle replacement than the one that afternoon in Boston four months earlier, but it was nonetheless as humiliating to Jackson, just as much of a slight and an embarrassment for Jackson not to be playing in such an important game. And, to Reggie, it was deliberate.

"Billy slapping me down one more time," Jackson would say. "Fran Healy used to say to me, 'I don't know how you do it.'

"'What do you mean?' I said.

"'You read the paper every day, you hear the people rip you to death. Doesn't it bother you?'

"I said, 'What good's it going to do me?' I hit in the big spot every day. I had to hit the baseball. I had to figure out how to put a number on the scoreboard. I didn't have time to think about what somebody was saying. You had to produce. If not, you had to answer to George, the fans, the media. The good thing about being a good athlete is that as long as you still have your skills, as long as I had that bat in my hands, I always had the last word."

Over the years, all manner of charges were leveled at Martin, including, because of his problems with Jackson, the vilest of all: being a racist.

"Says who?" asked an incredulous Rod Carew. "I would dare anyone to confront me and tell me Billy was a racist. There's no way. No way at all. Billy stood up for all the Latin guys and black players on the Twins. One time we were on the bus, and one of the white players started yelling stuff and all of a sudden there was a lot of shoving with Tony Oliva and a couple of other guys, and Billy jumped in and stood up for us."

"I never thought Billy was a racist," said Jim Kaat. "In fact, just the opposite. He seemed to be a sympathizer of minorities. He got the most out of Rod Carew, César Tovar, and Tony Oliva in Minnesota, and in Detroit, Willie Horton loved playing for him. Some blacks and Latinos might not have trusted him because he lied to everybody, but he always had their back and seldom was critical of them."

The facts do not support the charges of Martin as a racist. He often numbered among his favorite players Cesar Tovar, Rod Carew, and Zoilo Versalles—Hispanics; and Willie Horton, Gates Brown, Rickey Henderson, and Willie Randolph—African-Americans. Martin also listed among his favorite players Thurman Munson, Harmon Killebrew, Ron Guidry, Graig Nettles, and Mike Hargrove—all white.

Among his least favorite players were Reggie Jackson and Elliott Maddox, but also Tim Stoddard, Ken Holtzman, Larry Gura, and Jim Sundberg.

If Billy Martin was prejudiced, it had nothing to do with race, color, or religion, but everything to do with a player's failure to give his manager 100 percent effort all the time or to place himself above the team. In those cases, Martin was an equal opportunity bigot.

Martin's rationale for sitting Jackson in the sudden-death fifth game of the 1977 American League Championship Series was that Jackson had been a mere 1 for 14 in the series and that Splittorff was a tough left-hander, the kind that gave Reggie trouble. For confirmation, Martin consulted Catfish Hunter, who had played with Reggie in Oakland.

"Reggie can't hit Splittorff with a paddle," Hunter said.

That was all Martin had to hear. Blair would start in right field, Jackson would be on the bench. But this was Reggie Jackson, a clutch player who always came up big in important games.

"I was surprised, shocked, hurt," Jackson would say later. "You've got to be down. The season was on the line, and I was on the bench. Your pride's hurt. But I didn't want to be a problem. Not then. The writers came around looking for me to make a scene, but I wasn't going to do it. What I told them was, 'The man says I'm not playing, I'm not playing. He shouldn't be concerned about Reggie Jackson. He should manage the game.'

"The easiest thing in the world would have been for him to leave me in the lineup and have me go 0 for 4. At the very least, he showed some guts."

"Guts" was something never lacking in Martin, the manager, but he also knew his decision would cause a stir. He knew George Steinbrenner would not approve. He knew he was taking a big gamble, putting his job on the line. He knew if it backfired, he would pay a heavy price, but he did what he believed was right. It was Billy one more time, having the courage of his convictions.

"As the manager, my job was to win that game," Martin said. "And I had to put the nine guys on the field who I believed had the best chance of winning that game. I thought playing Blair instead of Jackson gave us the best chance to win because Reggie wasn't hitting, and he never hit Splittorff well. Blair did, and he also gave us better defense. We had Ron Guidry pitching, and I figured he wouldn't give up many runs, so I wanted to put our best defensive team around him. It was nothing against Reggie personally. I always said I would play Hitler and Mussolini if I thought they would help me win a game."

The Yankees came to bat in the top of the eighth, trailing 3–1, down to their final six outs. Willie Randolph led off the inning with a single, and with three right-handed hitters—Thurman Munson, Lou Piniella, and Cliff Johnson—due up for the Yankees, that forced Royals manager Whitey Herzog to remove Splittorff and bring in right-hander Doug Bird.

Munson struck out, but Piniella singled, putting runners on first and second with Johnson scheduled to bat. Martin looked down his bench and made eye contact with Jackson.

"Reggie," he said. "Hit for Cliff."

Big game. Big spot. And Reggie Jackson had a bat in his hands. He ripped a single that scored Randolph to make it 3–2, and that's where it stood as the Yankees batted in the ninth. Blair justified Martin's decision by leading off the ninth with a single, igniting a three-run rally that gave the Yankees a dramatic, come-from-behind 5–3 victory and their second straight American League pennant under Billy Martin.

The victory celebration in the Yankee clubhouse was wild and raucous, champagne being sprayed all over the place. Martin spotted Steinbrenner, grabbed a bottle of the bubbly, and sneaked up behind the owner and emptied the contents of the bottle on The Boss's head.

"That's for trying to fire me," Martin said.

"What do you mean, trying?" Steinbrenner replied.

As sweet as the victory was, Martin knew it was hardly enough. He remembered that he had won the pennant the previous year but was swept by the Reds in the World Series. He knew his job would not be secure unless he could also bring home a World Series victory, which had eluded the Yankees for 15 years.

What Martin didn't know, what he couldn't even imagine, was that the man who would bring him that elusive championship was the man with whom he had battled in a Fenway Park dugout four months earlier. And he would do it with the most awesome power display in World Series history.

Reggie Jackson was back in right field and in the cleanup spot in Billy Martin's lineup for Game 1 of the World Series against the Los Angeles Dodgers in Yankee Stadium. Jackson helped the Yankees build a run with a bloop single in the bottom of the first after the Dodgers had scored twice in the top of the inning.

Jackson popped out in the third, walked in the sixth, and was hit by a pitch in the eighth when the Yankees scored twice and took a 3–2 lead. The Dodgers tied the score in the ninth to send the game into extra innings, the Yankees winning with a run in the bottom of the 12th. Ironically, the game-winning hit was an RBI single by Paul Blair, batting in Jackson's position after once again being sent in to replace Jackson in right field after the Yankees had gone ahead in the eighth inning.

In Game 2, Jackson was hitless in four at bats, two strike-outs, a fly out, and a double play in the Dodgers 6–1 victory that evened the Series at one game apiece.

The Yankees won Game 3 in Los Angeles, 5–3. Jackson singled and walked in four plate appearances and drove in his first run of the Series in a three-run first.

Jackson hit his first home run of the Series in Game 4, a solo shot in the sixth for New York's final run in a 4–2 victory that gave them a three games to one lead in the Series, one victory away from their first world championship since 1962.

The Dodgers stayed alive by thrashing the Yankees, 10–4, in Game 5, a victory that rendered meaningless back-to-back home runs by Munson and Jackson (they shook hands after Thurman's blast) in the eighth inning. If nothing else, home runs in two straight games raised Jackson's confidence and convinced him that he had regained his long-ball stroke as the teams returned to Yankee Stadium for Game 6 on the night of October 18.

The Dodgers sent a pall over the Yankee Stadium crowd of 56,407 by scoring two runs in the top of the first, but in the bottom of the second, Jackson led off with a walk and scored on Chris Chambliss's home run that tied the score, 2–2.

The Dodgers scored a run in the third, but Munson led off the bottom of the fourth with a single, and Jackson stepped to the plate against Burt Hooton. He swung at Hooton's first pitch and hit a vicious line drive into the right field seats to give the Yankees a 4–3 lead.

As he circled the bases, the television camera focused on Reggie's face, and he looked into the camera and mouthed "Hi, Mom" twice. Then he ducked into the jubilant Yankee dugout, where the first to greet him was Martin, who patted the slugger on the cheek.

In the bottom of the fifth, after Mickey Rivers singled, Randolph bunted into a force out, and Munson lined out to center field, Jackson faced relief pitcher Elias Sosa. Again he attacked the first pitch and again hit a vicious line drive headed for the right field stands. He had to wait as the ball hooked toward the foul pole, but it disappeared inside the pole in fair territory to give the Yankees a commanding 7–3 lead. And Jackson was not finished.

He led off the bottom of the eighth against a third Dodgers pitcher, knuckleballer Charlie Hough. One more time, Jackson struck at the first pitch, but this time there was no doubt, the ball soaring deep into the Bronx night, deep into the seats in right center field.

Starting with his final at bat in Game 5, Jackson had hit four consecutive home runs in four consecutive official at bats, on four pitches, against four different pitchers. His three home runs in one game tied a World Series record set by Babe Ruth in 1926 and repeated in 1928. His five home runs were a World Series record. And he would be dubbed "Mr. October" by, of all people, Thurman Munson, who sought Jackson out after the game and said, "I can't believe what a great performance you put on tonight."

As Jackson whirled around the bases, the crowd chanted, "Reggie . . . Reggie . . . Reggie . . . ."

Rounding third base and heading for home, Jackson blew kisses at the press level of Yankee Stadium, in the direction of the owner's box. When Jackson reached the Yankee dugout, waiting for him there, ready to throw his arms around the slugger and embrace him was Billy Martin.

"I looked at that day as finally being accepted, or the reason why I had been brought to New York by George," Jackson said. "He had been singled out, and I was supposed to be his guy, so I looked at that day as together, we came through. I looked at it as that's the reason we're here, the reason we did this. That night, I became the player I thought I was.

"When I hit the ball out of the ballpark, I knew I held the World Series record, and that was cool.

"What defines [Bill] Russell? Championships! Getting ready to play. What defines [Joe] Montana? Championships! What defines [Michael] Jordan? There's all the same words, dedication, sacrifice, drive. The common thread is championship. Thank goodness I'm one. Thank goodness."

"Reggie Jackson is what I call a deliverer," said George Steinbrenner. "He's a winner. Everywhere he ever went he was a winner. He was great for me. There wasn't enough mustard in the world to cover him. He's still that way, and I love it. He was a great competitor, a big hot dog, but you loved that about him if you understood him, and he'd always deliver for you."

Some three hours after the 8–4 victory was complete, after the World Series was over, after the cheering had subsided and the crowd had left, after the champagne had been splashed in the winners' clubhouse, after most of the reporters and cameras and players had departed, Reggie Jackson was still basking in the glow of his remarkable performance. It was as if he didn't want to leave, didn't want the night to end. He wanted to stay in the ballpark and savor his moment.

Still dressed in his uniform pants, Jackson walked into the manager's office and plopped himself on a couch.

"I hit three home runs tonight," he said. "Do you realize that? Three home runs!"

"Yeah," said Billy Martin, feigning annoyance. "And you broke my record" (Jackson had six extra base hits, one more than Martin's record of five for a six-game World Series in 1953), "and that tees me off."

And then both men, who had battled so often during the season, began to laugh uncontrollably.

"Billy Martin," Jackson said. "I love the man. I love Billy Martin. The man did a hell of a job this year. There's nobody I'd rather play for."

"Next year," Martin said, "is going to be super."

"Weak is the man who cannot accept adversity," Jackson said. "Next year we're going to be tougher, aren't we, Skip?'

"You bet we will," Martin agreed. "We'll win it again next year."

"Yes, we will," Jackson affirmed. "We'll win because we have a manager who's feisty and I'm feisty, and we're going to be tougher next year. I'll go to the wall for him, and he'll go to the wall for me, and if anybody clashes with us, they're in trouble."

Twelve

SPLITSVILLE

George Steinbrenner was pleased. He had made good on his promise to return the Yankees to baseball supremacy. He had delivered two American League pennants and one World Series victory, and he had done it within his prescribed four-year period, another promise.

He had become a New York hero, rubbing elbows with celebrities like Cary Grant, Frank Sinatra, Bob Hope, Barbara Walters, Richard Nixon, and Henry Kissinger. In fact, Steinbrenner was a celebrity himself. He was received warmly in New York's chicest restaurants and bistros. One night, soon after the World Series, he entered the "21" Club, and the other diners greeted him with applause.

He had been vindicated in his decision, against his manager's objections, to sign Reggie Jackson as a free agent. He had challenged his manager, threatened him, and, in the end, showed Billy Martin who was The Boss.

George Steinbrenner was pleased, but he wasn't satisfied. He wanted more, and toward that end he opened his checkbook again and signed two more free agents for the 1978 season, doling out $1.1 million for five years to right-handed pitcher Rawley Eastwick and $2.8 million for six years for relief pitcher Rich "Goose" Gossage, the prize of the free agent class who had won 11 games and saved 26 for the Pirates, had an earned run average of 1.62, and 151 strikeouts in 133 innings. At 6 feet, 3 inches tall and 200 pounds, Gossage could throw as hard as 98 miles an hour, and with his Fu Manchu mustache (mustaches were acceptable under Steinbrenner's edict; beards, long hair, and huge Afros were not), Gossage was the most intimidating pitcher in the major leagues.

Like his boss, Billy Martin also was pleased. He arrived in spring training happier and more secure than he had been in years. He had brought the Yankees their first world championship in 15 years. He was idolized by thousands of Yankee fans, a hero in the greatest city in the world. He had patched up his differences with Jackson, and his relationship with Boss Steinbrenner was the best it had been. Martin believed that Steinbrenner had finally recognized his genius as a manager who fully deserved the adoration showered on him by his legion of fans.

Martin had overcome several obstacles in the previous two seasons, yet there remained some question if he could conquer his fatal flaw for self-destruction. His history showed that the more he won, the more secure he felt, the more defiant, stubborn, dictatorial, and difficult to handle he became. It happened in Minnesota. It happened in Detroit. And it happened in Texas.

Martin's first challenge in 1978 would be trying to keep both his new reliever, Gossage, and his old one, Sparky Lyle, happy. The manager convinced himself that this two-headed monster could work. He would alternate them as closers and use the pitcher who was not closing as a set-up man. Convincing Lyle, who had won 13 games in 1977, saved 26, and became the first relief pitcher ever to win the Cy Young award, was another matter.

Lyle, who came to the Yankees in a trade with the Boston Red Sox in 1972, was an outstanding relief pitcher and a valuable weapon for the Yankees, a pioneer in a baseball renaissance, the emergence of the "closer." He possessed a trademark handlebar mustache and a knee-buckling slider.

Lyle pitched for 16 years, won 99 games, saved 238, and, according to Graig Nettles, "did it all without ever throwing a fastball."

In addition to his pitching prowess, Lyle was one of the most popular Yankees of his, or any other, day, a fun-loving, practical-joking free spirit and clubhouse clown who had a penchant for stripping naked and sitting on birthday cakes that occasionally were sent to Yankees players.

Once, after completing a sweep of the White Sox in Chicago, the Yankees were waiting on their bus to take them to O'Hare Airport when an attractive young woman climbed onto the bus and asked the players for autographs.

"You don't have any paper," one Yankee said. "Where do you want us to sign?"

"Right here," she said as she pulled down her jeans and revealed her bare bottom.

The players were happy to oblige. When Lyle was asked if he was among them, he said, "Yeah, I signed 'Albert Walter Sparky Lyle Junior.'"

When pitchers and catchers reported to spring training in 1978, Lyle was missing, officially classified a holdout. Lyle never liked spring training. In 1974, on his way to camp, he stopped off and had a Fort Lauderdale doctor friend fit him with a total body cast and then made his way to Fort Lauderdale Stadium. When rookie manager Bill Virdon saw his ace relief pitcher in a cast, he almost had heart failure.

This time, however, Lyle's absence was seen as a fit of pique over the possibility of losing his closer's role to newcomer Gossage. When he finally agreed to terms and arrived at the Fort Lauderdale airport, he was greeted by a local high school band and cheerleaders with pom-poms that had been engaged by Steinbrenner. Lyle's reaction was to arrange the cheerleaders in a conga line and dance them through the airport. But he remained pessimistic about his immediate future.

"I knew it [the dual closer plan] wasn't going to work," said Lyle, who the previous season had pitched in 72 games, the most in the league. "There wasn't going to be enough work for both of us, and I was going to be the guy left out. I knew that if I pitched in fewer games, I wouldn't be as effective. The more I pitched, the better I got."

Martin's two-headed reliever system, and the season, got off to a rocky start. The Yankees opened on the road and lost four of their first five games in Texas and Milwaukee, and Gossage was the losing pitcher in two of them.

The Yankees returned to Yankee Stadium for the home opener against the White Sox on April 13, a day in which Jackson's boast—"If I played in New York, they'd name a candy bar after me"—became a reality when Standard Brands distributed "The Reggie Bar" to all fans entering the stadium.

"Why did they name a candy bar after him?" wondered Graig Nettles. "There already is one named after him—'Butterfingers.'"

As for the new candy bar, Catfish Hunter said, "When you open it, it tells you how good it is."

If Jackson was cocky and bombastic, Hunter, by contrast, was the most self-effacing, unassuming, and unpretentious of superstars. While Jackson arrived with a roar, Hunter blended in seamlessly and unobtrusively.

A humble and hard-working North Carolina farmer, he was more comfortable with the clubhouse attendants than he was with his millionaire teammates. Often, he would give the hired help a hand in cleaning the clubhouse, shining shoes, and loading and unloading the luggage truck for a trip. In spring training, rather than take a room in the team's plush hotel headquarters, Hunter often slept in the clubhouse, arising and helping prepare for the day's activities.

On the day his candy bar debuted, Jackson, in typical showman's fashion, blasted a three-run home run in the first inning and sent the Yankees on their way to a 4–2 victory that started them on a three-game winning streak. But the winning would not last very long.

On April 19, the Yankees and Blue Jays met in Toronto and went into the bottom of the ninth inning tied, 3–3, as Gossage prepared to start his fourth inning in relief. With one out and a runner on second, Gossage fielded a comebacker and threw the ball past first baseman Chris Chambliss, into short right field, allowing the winning run to score. It was the Yankees sixth defeat in 11 games, and Gossage had been the losing pitcher in three of them

"It was cold that day in Toronto, about 45 degrees, but with the wind chill factor, it felt like below zero," remembered Bucky Dent. "It was freezing, and Goose threw the ball away and we lost. [Graig] Nettles came off the field from third base, and as he passed Gossage, he said, 'Thata way to take one for the team, Goose.' We came home, and in our next game, Billy went to the mound to make a pitching change. He signaled for Goose, and

Mickey Rivers got in the bullpen car and started yelling, 'No, no, don't bring him in.'"

Said Gossage: "I was really awful in those first few weeks. I would get to the mound, and Thurman would look at me with that silly grin on his face and say, 'How are you going to lose this one?' I'd say, 'I don't know; get your ass back there, and we'll find out.'"

By the first week of July, the Red Sox were on a tear, the Yankees were in a free fall, 10 games behind Boston in the standings, and Steinbrenner was on the warpath, threatening, demanding, accusing, with his manager his principal target.

Gabe Paul had left the Yankees before the season to take over as president of the Cleveland Indians. To replace him, Steinbrenner brought in one of his Cleveland heroes, Al Rosen, an outstanding power-hitting third baseman for the Indians who was voted the American League's Most Valuable Player in 1953, and a contemporary and opponent of Billy Martin.

"It's not going to be easy for Billy to look Al Rosen in the face and say, 'What do you know about baseball?'" Steinbrenner said.

It might not have been easy, but Rosen's credentials as a player did not absolve him in Martin's eyes when Rosen, without informing his manager, called up minor league catcher Mike Heath. When Rosen did call Martin in the manager's office to tell him of the move, Martin hung up the phone on him.

Martin would dodge another bullet when Steinbrenner, upset when the Red Sox inflicted an early KO on a young pitcher named Jim Beattie, accused Beattie of being too soft and ordered him immediately sent to the minor leagues without consulting the manager. Martin vented his feelings to the press, and when Steinbrenner was told of the remarks, he exploded. "I'm not going to put up with this much longer," he said.

Once again, as they had in the recent past and as they would in the near future, the writers were on "Billy Watch," anticipating Martin's imminent firing. Instead, Martin met with Steinbrenner, who suggested some lineup changes. Martin had dropped a slumping Jackson out of the cleanup position, but he accepted the changes suggested, including returning Reggie to fourth in the batting order. Steinbrenner called their meeting one of the best he ever had with Martin. For emphasis, Steinbrenner told the press that Martin's job was safe "for this year. This should end the speculation that has been developing of late concerning Billy's job."

In the days following their July 13 meeting, Martin and Steinbrenner seemed to draw closer together. They even agreed to film a commercial for Miller Lite beer in which they feign an argument over the merits of the product.

"Less filling," says Steinbrenner.

"Better taste," counters Martin.

"Billy," Steinbrenner responds, "you're fired."

"Oh, no," says Martin. "Not again."

"George," observed Billy Martin Jr., "is a controlling man, but I don't think anybody ever could control my father. I get the sense a lot of people think there was theatrical drama going on, that they were acting parts and that behind the scenes they were sitting next to each other, having a beer and giggling about it all.

"There was a friendship between them. That friendship would turn sour at times. They were two men with large egos, and those kinds of people butt heads. There were times when I know Dad wanted to rip George's throat out. And then there were times when he wanted to give the man a hug. I think theirs was the classic definition of a love-hate relationship."

Reggie Jackson saw the relationship between Steinbrenner and Martin getting closer and sensed that he was losing favor with both his manager and his owner. Feeling insecure, Jackson sought an audience with Steinbrenner in an effort to repair the rift. Steinbrenner reassured Jackson that he was an important member of the team and that The Boss still had faith in Reggie's ability to get hot and help turn the season around.

In mid-July, the KC Royals came to New York and beat the Yankees in the first two games of a three-game series. Desperate to avoid a sweep, Martin took Steinbrenner's suggestion and inserted Jackson as the designated hitter in the No. 4 batting position on the night of July 17, which turned out to be a seesaw affair. After nine innings, the score was tied, 5–5. Jackson had failed to get a hit in four at bats, including a walk, and he was scheduled to be the second hitter in the bottom of the 10th.

Thurman Munson opened the inning with a single, and as Jackson came to bat, Martin flashed the bunt sign to third base coach Dick Howser, who, in turn, relayed it to Jackson.

Jackson was shocked. This was the ultimate insult, Martin flaunting his authority one more time. Reggie Jackson doesn't bunt; Reggie Jackson hits home runs.

Dutifully, Jackson squared to bunt the first pitch from reliever Al Hrabosky, known as "The Mad Hungarian" for his Fu Manchu mustache and his ritual of walking behind the mound, turning his back to the batter, bowing his head, talking to himself, then slamming the ball in his glove and turning around with a flourish to face the hitter.

"I threw the first pitch up and in," said Hrabosky, "and I took five steps at him and kind of challenged his manhood. 'Swing the bat,' I said. Obviously, the whole time, with his abilities and swinging in Yankee Stadium, I want him to bunt because I'm tough to bunt on."

With Reggie having tipped his hand by squaring around in bunting position with the first pitch, and noticing that the infielders were creeping in toward home plate, Martin removed the bunt and signaled to Howser that Jackson should hit away.

To be sure Jackson understood the sign, Howser called a time-out and walked toward home plate.

"He wants you hitting away," Howser told Jackson.

"I'm going to bunt," Reggie said defiantly.

On Hrabosky's next pitch, Jackson squared to bunt and missed the pitch completely for strike one.

Again Howser flashed the hit sign, and again Jackson squared to bunt and fouled it off.

One more time, Howser gave the hit sign, and one more time Jackson attempted to bunt and popped up to the catcher.

"The whole time, I'm standing there thrilled to death, him trying to bunt against me, because I'm respectful of the type of hitter he is," Hrabosky said. "He can take a checked swing and hit it out of Yankee Stadium."

"I was broadcasting at the time," said Fran Healy. "I knew the signs. I saw them take the bunt off, and I knew what was going to happen. After Reggie bunted and popped out, I remember him walking toward the dugout, and when he took his glasses off, he'da fought Mike Tyson. He was mad. And 'Stick' [coach Gene Michael] went down and told him to go inside, and Reggie said, 'Tell him [Martin] to tell me.'"

Martin was livid. When it was Jackson's turn to hit in the 11th inning, Martin replaced him with Cliff Johnson. When the Yankees lost the game in the 11th inning, the manager went berserk. Seething, he stormed into his office, picked up a clock radio, and smashed it against the floor. Then he grabbed an empty beer bottle and fired it against the wall.

Yankees vice president Cedric Tallis walked into Martin's office and closed the door behind him. Phone calls were placed to Al Rosen and to George Steinbrenner at his Tampa home. For once, Steinbrenner supported his manager completely. After a few minutes, the door to Martin's office opened, and the writers, who had been waiting outside, were invited in. The manager had an announcement.

"As of this moment," he said, "Reggie Jackson is suspended without pay, effective immediately, for deliberately disregarding the manager's instructions during his time at bat in the 10th inning. There isn't going to be anybody who defies the manager or management in any way. Nobody's bigger than the team. If he comes back, he does exactly what I say. Period."

Overlooked in this latest Martin–Jackson contretemps was defiance by Sparky Lyle, still smarting about being reduced from "closer" to set-up reliever. Called in to pitch in the fourth inning, Lyle pitched the fourth and fifth and then said, "I'm no long reliever. I'm going home."

So Lyle went home to New Jersey, and Jackson went home to Oakland. His suspension was for five days, during which time the Yankees went on a trip to Minnesota and Chicago.

The first day of Jackson's suspension was a day off on the team's schedule. On the second and third day, the Yankees swept a two-game series against the Twins. On the fourth and fifth days of the suspension, they beat the White Sox in Chicago.

Jackson returned to the team on July 23, the final game of a three-game series in Chicago, and was surrounded by a horde of reporters. When Martin asked what Jackson had said, he was told that Reggie showed no remorse for disobeying the manager and insisted he had done nothing wrong.

Jackson was not in the lineup against the White Sox. The Yankees won again, completing a three-game sweep. They had won five straight games without Jackson.

The July 23 game in Chicago was played in the afternoon, after which the Yankees would board their bus and head for O'Hare Airport for their charter flight to Kansas City. On the bus ride to the airport, Martin approached Murray Chass, a reporter for the *New York Times,* and said, "When we get to the airport, can I see you for a few minutes?"

When they arrived at O'Hare, Martin went to the reporter, and, still seething over Jackson's comments and his failure to offer an apology to his manager and teammates, he unburdened himself.

"I'm saying shut up, Reggie Jackson," Martin said. "We don't need none of your stuff. We're winning without you. We don't need you coming in and making all those comments. If he doesn't shut his mouth, he won't play, and I don't care what George says. He can replace me right now if he doesn't like it."

Chass asked Martin if he was speaking on the record, and the manager said he was. With that, Chass went to a telephone and called his office to report Martin's comments. Learning that the team charter would not leave for at least an hour, players, coaches, and manager did what they normally do while waiting at an airport—they repaired to the bar.

When it was time to board the charter, Martin walked along with Chass and another reporter, Henry Hecht of the *New York Post.*

"Did you get all that in the paper?" Martin asked Chass.

Told that Chass did, Martin was delighted, and his tongue perhaps loosened by drink, he continued to verbally berate Jackson.

"He's a born liar," Martin said. "They deserve each other. One's a born liar, the other's convicted."

There was no way to confuse Martin's use of the word *convicted*, a reference to Steinbrenner's 1974 felony conviction for making illegal contributions to Richard Nixon's reelection campaign. It was a gratuitous shot at The Boss, and it came out of the blue at a time when the relationship between Martin and Steinbrenner was on the mend. Steinbrenner had even given Martin his complete support in his decision to suspend Jackson. So why the attack on Steinbrenner?

While he was in Chicago, Martin had spent some time with Bill Veeck, the flamboyant, affable, and loquacious owner of the White Sox. After games, Veeck liked to hold court in the "Bards' Room," the White Sox press room. There, Veeck was always the center of attention, drinking beer, smoking his Newport cigarettes, flicking the ashes into a repository built into his wooden leg, and talking baseball. Usually he drew a crowd of baseball people, scouts, former players, executives, writers, and broadcasters, and, on this night, Billy Martin.

"I almost got you to manage my club," Veeck told Martin.

"What?"

"That's right. We would send Lemon [Bob Lemon, Veeck's manager at the time and a close friend and former teammate of Yankees president Al Rosen] to New York, and you would come here."

Martin couldn't believe what he was hearing. He was stunned. He would learn later that the proposed trade was not the brainchild of George Steinbrenner. In fact, Steinbrenner was opposed to the idea, and when it was suggested to him, he flatly turned it down. But listening to Veeck, Martin's knee-jerk reaction was that this was all Steinbrenner's doing. Presumably, it was that belief that prompted his "convicted" remark.

When Steinbrenner was told by Chass of Martin's remarks at O'Hare Airport, he was understandably stung.

"I don't know what to say," he told Chass. "I've got to believe that no boss in his right mind would take that."

And Steinbrenner, being in his right mind, knew what had to be done. This time, Martin had gone too far. This time, there was no making excuses for him, no saving his hide as George had done so often in the past.

"I told Billy that if he made that statement, George had every right in the world to fire him," said Martin's lawyer, Judge Eddie Sapir.

"I asked Billy if the job was affecting his health, and he said it was, so I told him I thought the best thing for him to do was call a press conference and say he was resigning for health reasons; that the job was affecting his health and because of that he didn't feel he could give the Yankees what he was committed and able to do under ordinary circumstances, and that it was in his best interest and the Yankees' best interest to resign. I told Billy that if he resigned for health reasons, it wouldn't be for cause, and his contractual obligation would remain in place."

When he got to Kansas City, Martin met with Mickey Morabito, the Yankees director of public relations, and the two worked into the wee hours composing Martin's resignation speech. The next morning, Morabito contacted the writers traveling with the team and told them there would be an important announcement at noon on the mezzanine level of the Crown Center Hotel, where the Yankees were staying.

An obviously distraught Martin showed up looking like he had not slept all night, which he hadn't. He wore dark glasses, his usual cowboy boots and jeans, and a short-sleeved shirt, a sweater draped over his back, with the arms of the sweater tied loosely at his chest.

When he spoke, his voice was husky and choked with emotion as he told the gathering he had a statement to make. Reading his prepared statement, Billy said, "I owe it to my health and mental well-being to resign at this time, and I am very sorry that there were things written about George Steinbrenner. He did not deserve them, nor did I say them. George and I have had our differences, and in most cases we have been able to resolve them."

Martin concluded his remarks by saying he would answer no questions because "Yankees don't throw rocks." Fighting back tears, he said, "I don't want to hurt the team's chances for the pennant with this undue publicity. The team has a shot at the pennant, and I hope they win it."

Martin went on to thank "the Yankee management, the press, the news media, my coaches, my players, and, most of all, the fans."

He barely got through his statement when he began to sob uncontrollably. Phil Rizzuto, Martin's friend and former Yankee teammate and now a broadcaster, moved in, put his arm around Martin, and walked him down the stairs and out the door of the hotel. Later that day, Martin left Kansas City, left the only job he ever wanted, and flew to Florida.

SPORTS FINAL
DAILY ◎ NEWS
★★★★
LARGEST
CIRCULATION
OF ANY PAPER
IN AMERICA
72
New York, Monday, October 29, 1979

Billy, you're fired!

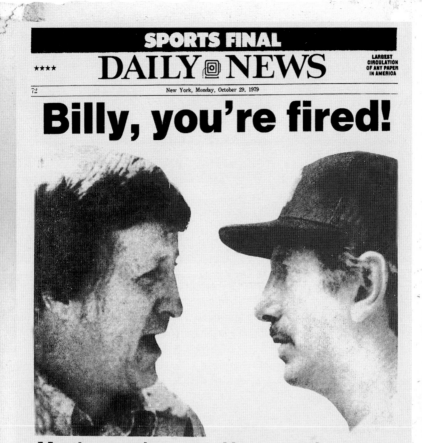

Martin punches out, Howser takes over

By PHIL PEPE

It was a case of one punch too many for Billy Martin, who became an ex-Yankee manager for the second time in 16 months last night. The news came in a brief statement from owner George Steinbrenner, who announced that Martin "will not be rehired for the 1980 season."

At the same time, Steinbrenner announced that former third base coach Dick Howser "has agreed to a multiple-year contract to manage the Yankees." Howser, who left the Yankees following the 1978 season to become head baseball coach at Florida State University, will be formally introduced as Yankee manager in a press conference Thursday. His contract runs through the 1982 season. Martin had a contract running through 1981.

Martin's demise came as a result of an incident in Bloomington, Minn., last Tuesday, when he was accused of slugging Joseph Cooper, a 52-year-old marshmallow salesman from Lincolnshire, Ill., in the lobby of a hotel. Martin denied hitting the man, who received 20 stitches in his lip the result, said Martin, of a fall. But Steinbrenner conducted his own investigation and presumably learned that Martin was more involved than he admitted.

STEINBRENNER HINTED that this time Martin might have gone too far when he said of the Bloomington incident. "I'm upset by it. Billy promised me he would not engage in any more fights. You just can't have this happening every two months. It's not good for the Yankee organization."

Martin found out that his days as Yankee manager had ended in a telephone call from a friend, Edward Sapir, a New Orleans judge.

Unable to contact Martin directly, Steinbrenner called Sapir and told him of his decision to replace Martin with Howser. Sapir then called Martin at his New Jersey apartment and gave him the bad news.

Martin took the news hard, just as he did when he tearfully announced his resignation in Kansas City on July 25, 1978. He was unavailable for comment and he told a friend he would have nothing to say about his firing.

"Yankees don't comment," Martin told the friend.

Steinbrenner extracted a promise of good behavior from Martin when he brought him back to manage the club this June, six months before planned. Martin had been forced into the resignation in Kansas City last year after calling Steinbrenner a "convicted liar."

THE YANKEE OWNER reconsidered

(Continued on page 33)

Giants hold off Rams
for 4th in row, 20-14
—Norm Miller, Page 52

Oilers trip Jets in OT
on Fritsch FG, 27-24
—Larry Fox, Page 55

The New York Daily News *could have kept this 1979 headline on hold. They would need it three more times after Billy Martin's second firing, following his punch-out of a marshmallow salesman.* COURTESY *NEW YORK DAILY NEWS*

George Steinbrenner often enjoyed a laugh with reporters. His moods were like the weather—if you didn't like one, all you had to do was wait a few minutes and it would change. That's me lower right, partly obscured by the shipping apparatus. COURTESY PHIL PEPE COLLECTION

Always a kid at heart himself, Billy Martin's tough guy demeanor softened when he was around kids. I had joined him at a charity luncheon when he took a liking to this young man and his sister. PHOTO BY CARL LOPRESTI/COURTESY BILLY MARTIN JR. COLLECTION

When he managed Billy Martin was often contemplative, sharply observant, and always with a fungo bat in his hand. PHOTO BY JOHN CORDES/NATIONAL BASEBALL HALL OF FAME LIBRARY, COOPERSTOWN, N.Y.

The looks on the faces of Billy Martin and George Steinbrenner tell you this was a coronation (one of the five times Martin was hired to manage the Yankees), not dethronement (one of the five times he was fired as manager of the Yankees). PHOTO BY ANTHONY PESCATORE/*NEW YORK DAILY NEWS*

This is not a dethronement but a somber moment in answer to a question at one of Martin's five hirings. PHOTO BY ANTHONY PESCATORE/*NEW YORK DAILY NEWS*

Thurman Munson (left) buried the hatchet and shook Reggie Jackson's hand after Jackson's first of three home runs in Game 6 of the 1977 World Series. PHOTO BY VINCENT RIEHL/*NEW YORK DAILY NEWS*

George Steinbrenner (center) loved coach Yogi Berra (left) and manager Billy Martin when the Yankees won the 1977 World Series. The good feelings were short-lived when Steinbrenner fired first Martin and later Berra as manager of the Yankees. PHOTO BY DAN FARRELL/*NEW YORK DAILY NEWS*

Here's another hiring (No. 3) with more promises of fidelity that would soon be broken.
COURTESY BILLY MARTIN JR. COLLECTION

To get Reggie Jackson to sign a free agent contract with the Yankees, George Steinbrenner "hustled me like a broad," Jackson said. PHOTO BY ANTHONY CASALE/*NEW YORK DAILY NEWS*

Billy's back as manager of the Yankees. To thousands of Yankees fans, Martin is "Forever #1," as it reads on his tombstone. COURTESY BILLY MARTIN JR. COLLECTION

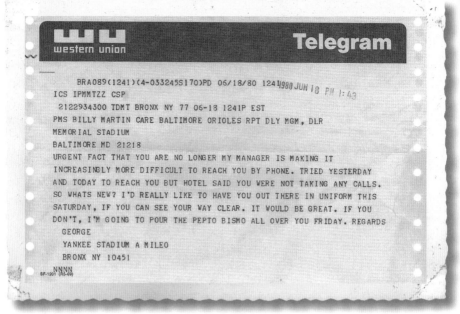

This 1980 telegram from George Steinbrenner to Billy Martin proves the two had a warm relationship filled with good-natured kidding—when Martin wasn't managing for Steinbrenner, that is. COURTESY BILLY MARTIN JR. COLLECTION

My son John, 14 at the time, had never put a fishing line in water until he met Billy Martin at Martin's home in upstate New York in August, 1989, just four months before Martin's death. COURTESY PHIL PEPE COLLECTION

Thirteen

RECONCILIATION

Despite their desperate position in the standings (a record of 55–45, in fourth place, eight games out of first) and the chaos swirling around them (Billy Martin was gone, Bob Lemon had replaced him), Saturday, July 29 was a festive occasion for the Yankees. It was another Old-Timers' Day at Yankee Stadium.

A crowd of 46,711 had turned out for a game against the Minnesota Twins and for the pregame ceremonies that would pay homage to Yankee heroes of the past. Phil Rizzuto was there and Whitey Ford and Mickey Mantle, 10 years into retirement but blond and fit and still looking powerful enough to drive balls into the upper deck. Also there was the Yankee Clipper, Joe DiMaggio, ready to take his customary place in the cleanup spot, the last to be introduced.

Broadcaster Frank Messer handled the day's festivities as master of ceremonies. First he introduced visiting dignitaries and Yankee officials. When he came to team president Al Rosen, the fans, who viewed the former Indians slugger as one of the villains of the piece in Martin's "resignation," let out a cascade of boos mixed with chants of "Billy . . . Billy . . . We want Billy . . . "

With his introductions completed and the crowd's applause subsided, Messer turned the crowd's attention to public address announcer Bob Sheppard "for two very special announcements."

"Ladies and gentlemen, your attention please," intoned Sheppard in his familiar stentorian voice. "The Yankees announce today that Bob Lemon has agreed to a contract to continue as manager of the Yankees through the 1978 and 1979 seasons . . . ."

Boos rained down from the rafters once again, louder than before, and signs appeared that read BILLY WILL ALWAYS BE NO. 1 and BRING BACK BILLY.

Undeterred by the interruption, Sheppard continued:

" . . . your attention to the rest of this announcement," he implored. "In 1980 Bob Lemon will become the general manager of the Yankees . . . "

More boos.

"Your attention, please," Sheppard pleaded. "Your attention, please . . . and the Yankees would like to announce at this time . . . introduce and announce at the same moment, that the manager for the 1980 season, and hopefully for many years after that, will be Number One, Billy Martin . . . "

For a moment, the crowd sat in stunned silence, in disbelief, as out of the Yankee dugout came the familiar, hunched figure in a Yankee uniform with the even more familiar No. 1 on his back. He trotted out with his cap in his hand, waving it to the adoring crowd, which was going wild. For more than seven minutes, the crowd cheered and shouted, stamped their feet, and yelled themselves hoarse, showering Martin with their applause, their love, and their affection.

This dramatic and unexpected turn of events was pure Steinbrenner theatrics, the scenario so obviously staged and choreographed by the Yankees owner. (Thirty years later, almost to the day, Steinbrenner, presumed to be in his dotage, apparently put his imprint on a similar surprise announcement, when Roger Clemens, standing in the owner's box, microphone in hand, revealed to a capacity Yankee Stadium crowd that he would be returning to the team later that season.)

Hours after Billy Martin had read his statement in Kansas City, George Steinbrenner began to have second thoughts. He had watched on television Martin's tearful "resignation" speech. (Steinbrenner knew the truth: It was a "resignation" because Steinbrenner allowed Martin to step down voluntarily rather than face the ignominy of being fired.) Steinbrenner would say later that he had been moved by Martin's remarks and his obvious contrition. He began thinking about it and realized Martin needed the Yankees, and the Yankees needed Martin.

Steinbrenner wasn't comfortable with how Martin's removal had gone down. He didn't like the feeling it left in the pit of his stomach. He wanted to make things right. Steinbrenner had a plan. He made a decision that wasn't entirely motivated by compassion and altruism. In the days following Martin's "resignation," the stadium switchboard had been flooded with calls from irate fans objecting to Martin's sudden departure, and Steinbrenner was concerned that those fans would boycott the Yankees if Martin was not there. Steinbrenner saw a chance to win over those fans and portray himself as the great and noble absolutionist by forgiving Martin and bringing him back.

To get his plan moving, Steinbrenner called Martin's agent, Doug Newton, who in turn telephoned Martin in Florida.

"Billy," Newton said, "he wants to bring you back as manager next year."

("I thought Doug was joking," Martin later said.)

"No," Newton insisted. "It's true. He wants us to meet with him in New York."

Martin flew to New York and joined Newton for their meeting in Steinbrenner's suite at the Carlyle Hotel. Steinbrenner had it all planned. The whole thing was his idea, including the date for the announcement, Old-Timers' Day, with a capacity crowd, a feeling of nostalgia, and many of Martin's former teammates and friends in attendance.

"It was the perfect time for George to spring his big surprise," Martin said. "We talked about a lot of things; how everything would be different this time. We promised each other that neither of us would talk about the other. We wouldn't deal with middlemen, we would go directly to the other if there were any problems. It was a good meeting. I was excited about what was to come.

"The one thing George warned me was not to say anything to anybody about his plan. He didn't want it to leak out. He wanted it to be a complete surprise, and I agreed. I was staying at the Sheraton Heights Hotel in Hasbrouck Heights, New Jersey, and Mickey Mantle, who had come in for the Old-Timers' game, came to stay with me. I didn't even tell him."

Steinbrenner's plan was for Martin to arrive surreptitiously at Yankee Stadium, enter through a side door, and be taken to a private room, where he would dress in his Yankee uniform and wait in a corridor for Bob Sheppard's announcement.

It was vintage George Steinbrenner, pure theater, and it came off like a charm, so perfectly that the announcement left most of the players and the Old-Timers stunned.

"I nearly fell off the bench," said Jim Spencer.

"Unbelievable," said Joe DiMaggio.

"I was shocked," said Reggie Jackson. "I felt like I had just been hit with a [Joe] Frazier left hook."

"I don't think it really shocked me or [Graig] Nettles or [Dick] Tidrow or Thurman [Munson]," said Sparky Lyle. "Billy had been hanging around for a while. All of a sudden, he popped up one day. I didn't know what he was there for. Billy never went anywhere or did anything if it wasn't for his benefit, and I don't mean that in a bad way. When I did find out, I said I figured something was up. That was my reaction. I was happy to see him back. He looked healthy, and I enjoyed playing for him. I used to like the way he took a bed check. He'd look in the room and say, 'Yeah, the bed's here.'"

The Yankees beat the Twins that day, 7–5. Jackson, batting sixth (Lemon's lineup, not Martin's), singled twice and drove in a run.

In the days after the announcement, Martin made a point of staying away from the team. He remembered his feeling of embarrassment, outrage, and betrayal when Dick Williams showed up one day in 1976 in Steinbrenner's box, and he didn't want to inflict that same embarrassment on Lemon, who had been Martin's pitching coach in 1976 and who Martin both liked and respected.

While the Yankees made their run at the Red Sox, a newspaper strike had shut down all of New York's dailies. All controversies, if there were any, went unreported. Martin wished a similar situation had existed when he was the manager.

From afar, Martin kept tabs on the Yankees as they slowly and methodically whittled away at the Red Sox once seemingly insurmountable lead, cutting it from a high of 14 games in mid-July to 6½ on August 1, to 4 on September 6, then drawing even after a 4-game sweep of the Red Sox in Fenway Park, the so-called Boston Massacre.

He followed closely as the Yankees and Red Sox finished the regular season dead even and met in a one-game playoff on October 2 in Fenway Park, and he watched on television when Bucky Dent hit a three-run home run off Mike Torrez in the seventh inning and when Goose Gossage retired Carl Yastrzemski on a pop fly to Nettles for the final out of a 5–4 victory that gave the Yankees their third straight American League East title.

And Martin watched when the Yankees beat the Kansas City Royals for the third straight year in the American League Championship Series, three games to one, and beat the Los Angeles Dodgers in six games for their second straight World Series championship.

He heard Lemon being praised for his low-key demeanor and hands-off approach that turned the season around.

Would the Yankees have been able to accomplish as much if Martin were still their manager?

Martin had no doubt they would have. He pointed out that at the time of his "resignation," the Yankees had begun their comeback by winning five straight games.

Would Martin, who often pinch hit for Dent in similar situations, have allowed him to hit in the seventh inning of the playoff game with the Yankees down by two runs and two runners on base?

Martin was certain he would have, but if he didn't, he believed he would have found another way to win the game. He was convinced that if he had remained the Yankees manager, it never would have come down to a one-game playoff.

"My father felt that no matter what the odds were," said Billy Martin Jr., "no matter who he faced, no matter what opposition he had against him, he could win, that somehow he'd find a way."

Martin always had found a way to win. He also found a way to get into trouble, occasionally not of his own making. He spent the winter after the 1978 season making appearances, sometimes as a favor to a friend.

On one such occasion, he appeared in Reno, Nevada, to help Bill Musselman, coach of the Reno Bighorns of the Western Basketball Association. Martin's presence was designed to help bolster sagging attendance and Billy agreed to appear with the stipulation that he would not be available to the media.

After the game, Martin went to a local bar where he encountered a man he thought to be a fan. The man, Ray Hagar, was a Reno newspaperman who never revealed that fact to Martin. Soon, their conversation became heated and, inevitably, punches were thrown, most of them by Martin. Hagar filed suit against Martin, but withdrew the suit and settled for Martin's apology.

This one time, at least, George Steinbrenner had no comment on Martin's behavior. Billy was not the Yankees' manager, so he was not Steinbrenner's problem.

With three consecutive American League pennants and back-to-back World Series victories, the Yankees were sending out unmistakable and fearful signs to the rest of baseball that they were at the start of another dynasty to parallel their successes of the 1920s, '30s, '40s, and '50s.

Most of the championship cast, including Lemon, the laid-back, hands-off manager, would be in place for the 1979 season. The owner, however, was not about to rest on past laurels. He never could and never would. To augment what he already had, George Steinbrenner orchestrated three important face-changing deals.

Convinced that the two-headed relief system that had existed the previous year was not working, the Yankees swung a five-for-five trade with the Rangers on November 10, 1978, that sent the 1976 American League Cy Young Award winner Sparky Lyle to Texas and brought a young fire-balling left-hander named Dave Righetti to New York. The deal prompted the irrepressible Graig Nettles to quip that Lyle "went from Cy Young to Sayonara."

Three days later, Steinbrenner opened his checkbook and signed as a free agent Luis Tiant, a 37-year old, cigar-smoking Cuban right-handed pitcher whose acquisition would have a twofold benefit. Not only would "El Tiante" add his veteran presence to the staff, it would remove from their fiercest rivals a pitcher who had won 121 games in the previous seven seasons for the Red Sox.

Nine days after signing Tiant, Steinbrenner struck again. And again he succeeded in weakening a rival. He corralled as a free agent left-hander Tommy John, who had won 37 games in the previous two years for the Los Angeles Dodgers, the Yankees' opponents in each of the last two World Series.

With a potential starting rotation of John and Tiant to go along with Ron Guidry, Ed Figueroa, Don Gullett, and Catfish Hunter, Goose Gossage as their exclusive closer, and an offense spearheaded by Reggie Jackson, Thurman Munson, Mickey Rivers, Willie Randolph, Graig Nettles, Chris Chambliss, Lou Piniella, and Roy White, the Yankees, "the best team money could buy," were considered prohibitive favorites to win a third straight World Series.

After opening the season with consecutive defeats to the Milwaukee Brewers, the Yankees won seven of their next nine games and on April 19 were poised to take over first place by completing a three-game sweep of the Orioles in an afternoon game at Yankee Stadium. There was no panic in the Bronx when Jim Palmer beat the Yankees, 6-3, to avoid the sweep, but an incident in the Yankee shower room after the game would have more wide-ranging repercussions. It started with the sort of good-natured needling that had marked this Yankees team.

"Cliff Johnson wasn't catching that day, and he thought he should have been, so he was in a bad mood," Goose Gossage remembered. "He was bitching and moaning the whole day in the bullpen.

"When the game was over and we went into the clubhouse, I unrolled the tape that I had put on my socks to keep them from falling, rolled it up, and flung it at Cliff, who was at his locker, right across the way from mine. The ball of rolled up tape whizzed over Cliff's head and went into his locker. Just then, Reggie [Jackson] was walking by, and he said, 'Hey, Goose, how'd Cliff do against you in the National League?'

"I said, 'He couldn't hit what he couldn't see.' I was just joking. It wasn't meant as a knock on Cliff, but he was in a bad mood, and he took it wrong. I undressed and headed for the shower, but first I stopped at the urinal. Next thing I knew, Cliff was standing next to me and he said, 'Hey, do you think you can back that shit up?'

"I thought, 'This guy's serious.' Then he took my head, and he kind of slapped it and shoved it real hard. I came back and hit him in the chest with my elbow, and then I hit him six or seven times. I had him backed against the first stall in the bathroom, and when I stopped, he hit me on the top of my head a couple of times.

"Brian Doyle tried breaking us up, but he's just a little guy and he couldn't do it, so he went and got help, and guys came into the bathroom and broke it up. I started to walk away, and as I did, I said, 'You know, Cliff, you're just a lazy bleep,' or something like that. That's when Cliff came at me again and tackled me, and we both fell against the wall, and as I did, I put my right hand down to break my fall, and we both landed on it. Cliff weighed 235 or 240, and I weighed 230, and all that weight was on my thumb. My thumb had no chance."

X-rays showed a tear of the ulnar collateral ligament in the joint of Gossage's right thumb. He underwent surgery three days later, and the prognosis was that he would be sidelined for from six to eight weeks. The trade that sent Sparky Lyle to Texas did not look like such a good deal after all.

Without a bona fide closer, the Yankees blew late leads and lost games they should have won. They ended the month of April by losing six straight games, slipping below .500, and falling into fourth place, three and a half games out of first.

Before long, things began spinning out of control. Jogging in from right field, Reggie Jackson sustained a partial tear of the sheath of muscle in his left calf and would miss almost a month.

Graig Nettles suffered a series of minor injuries, and when he tried to play through them, his production declined. His batting average would dive from .276 to .253, his home runs would decline from 27 to 20, his RBI from 93 to 73.

When no other reliever stepped up to replace Gossage, Ron Guidry volunteered for the job, but after going seven days without pitching, he was returned to the starting rotation. His bullpen stint, albeit brief, appeared to have messed up his rhythm, and he could not duplicate his sensational 1978 performance when he was 25–3 with a 1.78 ERA, 248 strikeouts, and 9 shutouts. By the middle of July he had a record of 6–7.

On June 8, the Yankees embarked on a nine-game trip to Kansas City, Minnesota, and Texas. They won two out of three in Kansas City and the first of three in Minnesota, but when they lost four of their last five games on the trip, their record fell to 34–31 in fourth place, a season low eight games out of first.

George Steinbrenner decided something had to be done, and he knew just what that something was. The Yankees needed a change. They needed someone to light a fire under Steinbrenner's sagging ballclub; they needed a quick fix. And Steinbrenner had just the man to provide it: Billy Martin.

It had already been announced that Martin was to return in 1980, so Steinbrenner reasoned, why not bring him back six months earlier? Martin took over on June 19 with the Yankees in fourth place, eight and a half games out of first.

Billy II failed to produce the magic or the quick fix Steinbrenner hoped it would. The Yankees played better under him, but upon his return Martin found the team beset with too many problems to pose a serious challenge to the Orioles, who were running away in the AL East.

Not the least of Martin's problems was what to do about Thurman Munson, the captain and heart and soul of the team, who was plagued by painful knees as the result of years of squatting behind home plate. It had become apparent that Munson's days as a full-time catcher were behind him.

In addition to his physical problems, Munson was distracted by other thoughts. He had decided not to disrupt the schooling of his three children by having his family join him at his in-season home in New Jersey. But Munson knew his place was with his family. His children needed a father, and he would take advantage of every opportunity to go home to Ohio to be with his family if only for a few hours.

Munson began taking flying lessons in the winter between the 1977 and 1978 seasons and soon found in flying a way to escape the grind of the major league season. He purchased a small plane, a Cessna Citation, with one objective in mind: the freedom to fly home on days off and be with his family.

During spring training, Munson was interviewed on television by broadcaster Tony Kubek, the former Yankees shortstop, who asked the catcher about his flying.

"I think it's great," Munson said. "The feeling you get being alone for an hour or two. You're up there, and nobody asks any questions. You don't have to put on any kind of an act. You just go up there and enjoy yourself. You have to be on your toes, but it's just a kind of relaxation when you spend a lot of time by yourself, and I need that. I also need to get home a lot, so I fly."

By July 6, the Yankees had slipped 10½ games out of first as they began a 10-game trip to Oakland, Seattle, and California. They swept four games in Oakland to cut the margin to eight games, but lost two out of three in Seattle and the first two in Anaheim, the last an 8–7 defeat in 12 innings.

After the game, I returned to the team's hotel and stopped in the hotel gift shop for something to read before retiring. There, I spotted Munson grabbing bags of snacks.

"What are you doing?" I asked.

"I didn't get a chance to eat," he explained. "I'm hungry."

"Don't eat that junk," I chided. "There's an all-night hamburger place up the street; why don't you go get something nutritious?"

"I don't like eating alone," he replied.

"I've got nothing to do," I said. "I'll go sit with you."

"You will?" he said, sounding surprised.

We spent more than two hours in the hamburger place, talking not about baseball, but about other things. Munson told me how much he missed being with his kids, and then he reiterated his passion for flying, the peace and serenity he found in the air.

"I'll take you up with me someday," he offered. "You'll see how peaceful it is."

"No way," I objected. "I'm not flying with you."

"There's nothing to worry about," he argued. "It's perfectly safe. Besides, I don't care if you live or die, but I do care if I live or die."

As July turned into August, the Yankees had fallen 14 games out of first place. The season, for all practical purposes, was lost. The Yankees were not scheduled on August 2, and Billy Martin took advantage of the day off to plan a fishing trip in New Jersey with his teenage son, Billy Joe. Munson flew home to Canton to spend time with his family and to practice takeoffs and landings in his Cessna Citation.

The director of public relations for the Yankees in 1979 was Mickey Morabito. On the morning of August 2, he was at his desk when he was summoned to George Steinbrenner's office. Morabito had learned that a summons by The Boss usually meant he was about to be rebuked for a newspaper article that was unfavorable to Steinbrenner. Not this time.

"When I walked into George's office, he was in a somber mood," said Morabito. "He waited until everybody had gathered—there were about five or six of us—then he said, 'I've got some bad news. We lost Thurman today.'

"Somebody said, 'What do you mean, we lost Thurman?'

"Then George told us that Thurman had been killed when his plane crashed in Canton as he was practicing takeoffs and landings. Everybody was in a state of shock, near tears.

"Then George said to me, 'Go find Billy Martin and give him the news.'"

"I knew Billy was fishing somewhere on the Jersey shore. I didn't know where exactly, but he had given me a phone number for the harbormaster. I walked out of George's office, and right outside his office is the receptionist's desk and the switchboard, and I just picked up the receptionist's phone and made a call.

"I got the harbormaster and told him to get Billy off the boat, it was an emergency. I waited a long time, and then I heard Billy's voice on the line and I told him the news. At first, he didn't believe me. 'No,' he said. 'It's not true.'

"I convinced him that it was true by telling him all the details I had gotten from George, and Billy just started to sob. He was crying like a baby. I don't remember Billy saying good-bye. He just kind of ended the conversation by hanging up the phone without a word, that's how broken up he was."

"I was looking forward to the day," Billy Martin Jr. said. "So was Dad. He loved to fish. The team was going bad, and this was a way for him to get some rest and relaxation and for us to spend some quality time together.

"Nick Nicolosi, his friend from the Sheraton Heights Hotel, had made all the arrangements. There were just the three of us, but Dad kept ripping Nick because the fishing was lousy. Dad was cursing Nicolosi with every cast.

"All of a sudden, we heard the bullhorn.

BILLY MARTIN, COME TO THE DOCK . . . BILLY MARTIN, TO THE DOCK PLEASE . . . "

"And Dad said, 'What did I do now?'

"We got to the dock, and there were two police cars waiting there. One of the policemen said, 'We have an emergency phone call for you,' and Dad got in one of the police cars and drove off. Nick and I followed in the second police car.

"The call was from Mickey Morabito, who told Dad what had happened. When he hung up with Morabito, Dad called Diana Munson, Thurman's wife, and talked with her. Then we left and went back to his apartment in New Jersey. Dad started to cook some steaks, and he said, 'I gotta go out.'

"I said, 'You can't go out tonight, Dad.'

"He said, 'What do you mean?'

"I said, 'If you go out tonight, you're going to be all upset. You're liable to drink too much, and somebody's going to say something, and you're going to have a real short fuse. You don't want to bash Thurman's memory.'

"'You're right,' he said.

"I told him I'd pour him scotch all night if he wanted me to, so I fixed him a big Chivas Regal on the rocks, and he never touched a drop. We sat there and ate steaks and watched two John Wayne movies, and he burst into tears two or three times."

Munson's funeral was held in Canton on Monday, August 6. George Steinbrenner had provided a charter plane that transported Yankees executives, office workers, Martin and his coaches, the entire team, some accompanied by their wives, several umpires, and members of the media to Canton. During the service, Martin wept uncontrollably for the departed captain.

"Billy was such an emotional guy, and he loved Thurman," said Morabito. "I think in Thurman, Billy felt he had an ally in his battles with Reggie and George."

Not only did Martin consider Munson an ally, but Billy, who was notorious for second-guessing and verbally abusing catchers, exempted Munson from such treatment. He demonstrated explicit faith in Munson's judgment and he appreciated him as a selfless player who always put team ahead of self, and as a winner and a guy who played hard and played hurt.

Martin liked Munson's competitive fire. Just as Casey Stengel saw himself in Martin, Martin saw himself in Munson, a player who performed his best in clutch situations, a player he considered "a true Yankee," a throwback to the Yankees of Martin's era and one Martin deemed worthy of wearing the pinstripes. To Billy, there was no higher praise.

Martin knew Munson's desire, his drive, and his leadership were irreplaceable and that without him, the Yankees would not be the same.

At the time of Munson's death, the Yankees were buried in fourth place, 14 games out of first, but any hope they could take a run at the first-place Orioles faded. The joy of playing, the fire and the fight, were sucked out of the Yankees and their manager with Munson's demise. The Yankees would sleepwalk through the next weeks and end the season by winning their last eight games.

It was too little, too late as the Yankees finished the season 13½ games out of first place. The late spurt gave Martin hope for the immediate future. He vowed to himself, and to those close to him, that things would change in 1980. He rationalized that coming back midway in the season, with the team already eight games out, was too much to overcome. He often preached that he needed to be with his team from the first day of spring training to implement his program and set the tone for the season. Next year, he promised, things would be different.

Who would ever have guessed that pugnacious, intrepid, brawling, battling Billy Martin would be taken down by the Marshmallow Man?

Fourteen

BILLYBALL

Putting Billy Martin in a bar is something akin to walking into a refinery with a lighted match. There's likely to be a hell of an explosion.

It happened in Detroit. It happened in Reno, Nevada. It happened in Baltimore. It happened in Arlington, Texas. And it happened in Bloomington, Minnesota, on the night of October 23, 1979, just 24 days after the end of the baseball season.

Martin had spent the days after the season at his New Jersey apartment, catching up with some chores, playing some golf, visiting with friends, and avoiding watching the American League Championship Series between Baltimore and California on television. If he wasn't in it, he wasn't interested.

As the World Series between the Orioles and the Pittsburgh Pirates was beginning, Martin was on an airplane headed for Minneapolis to visit his longtime friend from his days with the Twins, restaurateur Howard Wong. They would spend a few days in Minnesota before driving to South Dakota to hunt pheasant.

On October 23, Martin and Wong returned to Minneapolis from their hunting trip. Billy, looking relaxed and rested, was in good spirits. He had reservations later that day for a flight to

Dallas, where he would hook up with his buddy Mickey Mantle for a few days of golf.

The trip from South Dakota to Minnesota took longer than he figured, and Martin realized he would miss his flight. He called Mantle and said he would book another flight later in the week, and he asked Wong to get him a hotel room near the airport in Bloomington. While Martin dined in Wong's restaurant, his friend Howard worked the phones but returned with bad news. A beautician's convention had tied up the area. There were no rooms to be had.

Determined, Wong got back on the telephone and returned to inform Martin that he had managed to find Billy a room in the swanky Hotel de France, Bloomington's finest and most expensive hotel.

After dinner, at about 9:00 p.m., Wong drove Martin to the hotel, helped Billy check in, and said, "I'll take you to the airport tomorrow."

"It's early," said Martin. "Let's go downstairs and have a drink first."

"All right," Wong agreed, "but just one. I'm tired."

The two men repaired to the hotel bar and ordered a drink. They reminisced about the wonderful time they had had in South Dakota, ordered more drinks, talked some more, and ordered more drinks. While they were drinking and talking, two men walked into the bar and took seats near Martin and Wong.

What happened next is a matter of he said/he said.

This is the version of Joseph Cooper, a 52-year-old, 6-foot, 210-pound salesman from Lincolnshire, Illinois, who was in town on a business trip:

Cooper said he recognized Martin and engaged him in baseball talk. They talked about the Yankees, and then Cooper said,

"I think Dick Williams [who had managed the Montreal Royals that season] did a good job this year. He deserved to be manager of the year in the National League. And so did Earl Weaver in the American League."

"Dick Williams is an asshole," Martin replied. "They're both assholes, and so are you for saying it."

After a few minutes, Martin asked the man, "What do you do for a living?"

"I'm a salesman," said Cooper.

"What do you sell?"

"Marshmallows."

"Marshmallows!" shrieked Martin, bursting into laughter.

"Yeah, everybody thinks it's funny, but I make a good living at it."

"You're still an asshole," Martin replied.

At that point, according to Cooper, Martin reached into his pocket, pulled out a roll of bills, and said, "Here's $500 to your penny I can knock you on your ass."

Cooper went into his pocket, took out a penny, placed it on top of the five $100 bills Martin had put on the bar, and said, "Let's go."

According to Cooper, he got off his seat and walked out of the bar toward the hotel lobby, and Martin followed him. The next thing he knew, Cooper said, he was smashed in the mouth with a right hand and found himself on the floor, bleeding from his lip.

Martin's version, as detailed in his autobiography, *Number 1,* differs from Cooper's.

According to Martin, he and Wong arrived at the hotel at nine o'clock that night and repaired to the bar where they ordered drinks. After a few minutes, they were approached by two strangers, one of whom was a burly fellow whom Martin judged to be about two hundred and thirty pounds.

The big fellow introduced himself to Martin as Joseph Cooper. Martin introduced himself and then introduced his companion, Wong.

Cooper seemed star-struck to be in the company of a celebrity and wanted to talk baseball with the Yankees' manager. At one point, Cooper said, "You know, you didn't deserve to be manager of the year. Earl Weaver or Dick Williams did."

Bad move!

Martin asked Cooper what he did for a living and was told that Cooper was a marshmallow salesman.

"Well, maybe you're not the best marshmallow salesman," Martin replied.

As the conversation continued, Martin started to get an inkling that Cooper was looking to pick a fight. His suspicions were confirmed when Cooper said, "You're the little guy who gets in all those fights, aren't you?"

Martin said he was and Cooper responded with a challenge.

"I can lick you," Cooper said. "I bet I can lick you."

"You can't," Martin replied, "and I don't even want to talk about it."

Cooper persisted.

"You don't look like you're big enough to be a fighter," he said.

"I'm not too big," Martin said, "but I don't think size is important. Big guys go down as easily as little guys."

Unable to dissuade his tormentor, Martin issued a challenge of his own. He reached into his pocket and pulled out three hundred dollars, which he placed on the bar.

"Here's three hundred dollars to your penny you can't whip me," said Martin, and with that, Cooper and his buddy walked out of the bar. Martin figured he had scared off the marshmallow salesman and put an end to the unpleasantness, but moments later Cooper returned, put a penny on the bar and said, "I thought it over, and the odds are too good to pass up."

Cooper proceeded to remove his jacket. "Let's get it on," he said.

"You're serious, aren't you?" Martin said.

"Yeah, I'm serious," Cooper said.

Martin suggested they step outside and Cooper agreed.

Martin left the bar, intending to cross the lobby to the elevator and go to his room. Cooper followed closely behind.

According to Martin, Cooper insisted that they rumble and Martin knew he had reached the point of no return when Cooper grabbed his right shoulder, spun him around and threw a left hand.

"I slipped his left," Martin said, "and hit him with a right hand. He went down like a sack of coal. He was out. I stood there looking down at him, and I was saying to myself, 'How in the hell did I get into this?'"

At that point, a hotel security guard arrived and told Martin to leave and that the guard would handle the situation.

Martin returned to the bar, picked up his three hundred dollars, said good night to Wong without telling his friend what had happened, and took the elevator up to his room.

Martin thought that was the end of it, but an anonymous caller tipped off the city desk of the *St. Paul Pioneer Dispatch* that Billy Martin had been in a fight with a marshmallow salesman at a Bloomington hotel. The story made its way to the Associated Press wire, and a telephone call from the Yankees director of public relations, Mickey Morabito, alerted Martin that the story was on page 1 of the *New York Post*. Together, Morabito and Martin composed a statement in which Martin admitted the altercation, but said the marshmallow salesman must have fallen because Billy never hit him.

George Steinbrenner wasn't buying any of it. It's interesting to recall that two years later, Steinbrenner, himself, would get involved in an altercation in a Los Angeles hotel elevator during the 1981 World Series between the Yankees and Dodgers. Two Dodgers fans had needled him, Steinbrenner said, and he had to put them in their place with an unavoidable physical confrontation. Single-handedly, he took care of both of the hecklers, Steinbrenner said. The two hecklers were never found, nor did they ever surface voluntarily. Now, in a similar situation, Steinbrenner refused to believe Martin's story and decided Billy had to go. He called Martin's attorney, Judge Eddie Sapir of New Orleans, and said Martin was finished.

"It seems to me this pattern is never going to end," said Steinbrenner, who told Sapir he worried what might have happened if the marshmallow salesman hit his head on the marble floor of the Hotel de France and was killed. "I don't want a Yankee manager being involved in a guy being killed."

Sapir tried pleading Martin's case. He asked Steinbrenner to talk to Billy and get his side of the story, but Steinbrenner refused. "I'm not going to talk to Billy at all," he said. "Billy's fired."

On Sunday, October 28, the Yankees released the following terse statement:

"Billy Martin has been relieved of his duties as manager of the New York Yankees, and Dick Howser has been named to succeed him effective immediately."

The official coronation came three days later in a lavish press conference at the Tavern on the Green in Central Park. Long-time third base coach Dick Howser would take over as manager of the Yankees in the 1980 season. At the same time, Gene Michael would become the Yankees general manager, replacing Al Rosen, who had resigned after the 1979 season because he could no longer tolerate Steinbrenner's meddling and second-guessing.

Sparky Lyle: "When you start talking about firing Billy Martin as manager of the New York Yankees, you might as well stab him with a knife."

The abrupt end of Billy II left Billy Martin shattered and disconsolate. It also left him unemployed, although Steinbrenner would make good on Martin's full salary of $125,000 a year for two years.

During his two terms as manager of the Yankees, the first for 471 games, the second for 96 games, whenever Martin would have his fill of Steinbrenner's many rantings, ravings, and threats to fire him, he would boldly proclaim, "If he fires me, I'll come back and beat him with another team."

He was about to get his chance.

Not long after getting the boot from George Steinbrenner, Martin got a phone call from Charles O. Finley, the maverick owner of the Oakland Athletics

"Billy," Finley roared, "I want you to come and manage my ballclub."

After several weeks of haggling over money with Finley, who was trying desperately to get Martin as cheaply as he could, a deal was struck on a three-year contract for $125,000 a year, with Steinbrenner kicking $150,000 into the pot. Paramount to Martin was that he would have total control over player personnel.

Finley was in the process of trying to sell his team, and, consequently, he was running his operation on a shoestring.

"Charlie was upfront with me," Martin said. "He told me he wasn't going to get me any players. He admitted his team was bad and that he refused to do anything to help me, not out of spite but because he was going to sell the team anyway, and he didn't want to spend any more money than he had to.

"'You're not going to have this and you're not going to have that,' he told me.

"'That's all right, Charlie,' I said. 'I'll do the best I can with what I have.'"

There were many reasons that managing the A's was appealing to Martin, not the least of which was that it was near his hometown, close to where his mother, Joan, lived. She was aging, and Billy saw it as an opportunity to spend some time with her in her declining years.

Professionally, it was a chance to get back in uniform without missing a beat, an opportunity for the first time in his managerial life to have complete authority on player moves, and, best of all, a challenge that Martin found irresistible, to take a team in the depths and turn it around.

Less than 10 years after they had been a baseball dynasty by winning five straight division championships and three straight World Series, the A's had fallen on hard times, largely because of Finley's stinginess. He refused to pay his star players, who walked away from Oakland as soon as they had gained free agency, and he refused to sign other free agents to replace those he had lost.

In 1979, the year before Martin arrived, the A's finished with a record of 54–108, last in the American League West, 34 games out of first, and drew only 306,763 paying customers all season.

"Now, remember, Billy," Finley warned as spring training approached, "you have a bunch of kids who can't play."

"That's all right, Charlie," Martin replied confidently. "I'll mold them. I'll make them into ballplayers."

Among the "kids who can't play" that Martin inherited were Rickey Henderson, who improved his batting average from .274 to .303, his runs from 49 to 111, and stolen bases from 33 to 100; Tony Armas, who went from 11 homers and 34 RBI to 35 homers and 109 RBI; Mike Norris, who went from 5 wins to 22; Rick Langford, who went from 12 wins to 19; and Matt Keough, who improved from 2 wins to 16.

Employing a dashing style of play that would be dubbed Billy-Ball, the Athletics dazzled the opposition with speed and daring.

"I liked working for Finley," Martin said. "He was the only owner who never bothered me. Can you believe it? This man who had a reputation for changing managers like he changed shirts, for telephoning the dugout during a game and telling his managers what moves to make, never bothered me. Not once.

"He never came to the games. He stayed in Chicago running his insurance business, or at his home in Indiana, and he would listen to the games on the radio and call me every once in a while. One day he heard that we stole eight bases in a game, and he couldn't believe it.

"'You stole eight bases today?'

"'That's right, Charlie.'

"'You stole home twice?'

"'Yeah, Charlie.'

"'Jesus, how come you're not all excited?'

"'Because they're just playing good baseball, Charlie. What's to get excited about?'

"A couple of days later, we stole five bases, and he called me again.

"'You stole five more bases today? You guys are winning? What the hell is happening out there?'

"Finley just couldn't believe that we had such good players, that this was the same team he told me was going to be so bad."

In Martin's first season as manager, the Athletics won 83 games, 29 more than the previous year, and finished in second place in the AL West. Their attendance almost tripled, to 842,259.

Meanwhile, the Yankees won 103 games and captured the American League East by 3 games over Baltimore. But then, as now, winning a division title was not enough for George Steinbrenner. When the Kansas City Royals swept the Yankees in a three-game American League Championship Series, The Boss went on a familiar rampage.

On November 21, the press was called to Yankee Stadium and assembled in the office suite of George Steinbrenner. A table was set up with drinks, another with finger sandwiches, and Steinbrenner conducted a press conference that was right out of *Saturday Night Live*.

"Doesn't anybody want a sandwich?" Steinbrenner asked. "Nobody's eating the sandwiches. Aren't you hungry?"

Nobody moved, so Steinbrenner pressed on with the business at hand. He said that Howser had come to him and said he had a business offer in Florida land development that he could not refuse; therefore, he was stepping down as manager of the Yankees. His successor would be Gene Michael, who was leaving his job as general manager.

Howser, sitting at the head table a few seats away from Steinbrenner, said nothing. On his face was a wry smile; actually more smirk than smile.

Steinbrenner kept saying that Howser would be well rewarded for his years of service to the Yankees, who were paying the mortgage on his Florida home.

"Dick Howser will be well taken care of," Steinbrenner insisted.

To some, it seemed Steinbrenner was protesting too much. Finally, one impish writer said, "You don't have to convince us, George. I always said I have two ambitions in life: one, to be adopted by you, and two, to be fired by you."

The 1981 season would bring with it the longest labor strike in sports history. It began on June 12 and ended on August 10, erasing more than one-third of the season. In all, 713 games were lost.

With the resumption of the season, major league owners announced their plan for the playoffs. The season would be split into two halves, as follows: The teams in first place in each of the four divisions at the start of the strike would automatically qualify for the postseason and would play a best-of-five series against the winners of the second half (from the point of resumption until the scheduled end of the season) to qualify for the League Championship Series. The winners of the LCS would then play in the World Series.

Under this arrangement, the Athletics, by virtue of their "first half" record of 37–23, a game and a half better than Texas, and the Yankees, at 34–22, two games ahead of Baltimore, were assured a spot in the playoffs.

It was ironic that while Billy Martin had found stability in Oakland, the managerial merry-go-round ran amok in the second half of the strike-shortened season. When the season resumed, there were several managerial changes.

In Kansas City, the Royals had finished in fifth place in the first half with a record of 20–30. When they lost 10 of their first 20 games in the second half, manager Jim Frey was fired and replaced by Dick Howser (so much for George Steinbrenner's claim that Howser had left baseball voluntarily to avail himself of a wonderful opportunity in Florida land development), who rallied the Royals to beat out Oakland in the second half by a game.

After finishing two games ahead of Baltimore in the first half, the Yankees stumbled in the second half under Gene Michael, who was fired. To replace him, Steinbrenner reached out to an old reliable, Bob Lemon, who returned for his second tour of duty as manager. Although he could not turn the team around and finished in sixth place, five games out of first in the second half, Lemon rode the coattails of Michael's good work in the first half into the postseason.

It would be Lemon's Yankees against the Brewers in the East, and Martin's Athletics against Howser's Royals in the West— three-fourths of the 1981 American League playoff teams piloted by men who had managed for George Steinbrenner.

Martin guided his young A's to a three-game sweep of the Royals, while the Yankees battled the Brewers through five pressure-packed games. After winning the first two games, the

Yankees lost the next two to tie the series at two games each. After the fourth game defeat, Steinbrenner stormed into the Yankee clubhouse and let his team have it with both barrels.

Singling out Rick Cerone, Steinbrenner lashed out at the catcher for a costly base-running blunder in the 2–1 defeat. A tough, hard-nosed kid from Newark, Cerone could take it no longer and fired back.

"Fuck you, you fat son of a bitch," he said. "You never played the game. You don't know what the fuck you're talking about."

Suddenly, the room grew silent, until Steinbrenner punctured that silence by telling Cerone, "And you won't be playing this game as a Yankee next year."

The following day, when he arrived at the stadium for the deciding fifth game, Cerone found an envelope waiting at his locker. Inside was a note from Steinbrenner, who sort of, kind of apologized to Cerone and dismissed the catcher's outburst as frustration. The incident was forgotten, wrote Steinbrenner, who added a P.S.: "You better not make any base-running mistakes tonight."

The Yankees won the fifth game against the Brewers and advanced to the American League Championship Series against the Oakland Athletics. Now Billy Martin had his chance to make his boast come true that if George Steinbrenner "fires me, I'll come back and beat him with another team."

But it was not to be. Lemon's Yankees beat Martin's Athletics in a three-game sweep. To make matters worse for Martin, the most damage—6 hits in 12 at bats, a .500 average, 1 home run, and 9 RBI—was inflicted by one of Billy's boys, Graig Nettles, whom Martin had tutored in the minor leagues in Denver, schooled in Minnesota, and managed in New York.

Martin accepted his defeat with as much grace as Billy could muster—which usually wasn't very much—and looked forward to better days ahead in Oakland with a team that was improving.

Martin and the Athletics were riding high, but the problem with riding high is that it makes the fall from that perch that much more painful. And the Athletics fell in 1982 with a resounding thud. Martin had resurrected the Oakland franchise, brought excitement to the Bay Area with a team record home attendance of 1,735,489, but he also drew severe criticism for overworking his young pitching staff. Several of his pitchers came up with sore arms. Two years after winning 22 games, Mike Norris won only 7. Rick Langford fell from 19 wins to 11, Matt Keough from 16 to 11. Despite a major league record of 130 stolen bases for Rickey Henderson, the A's finished in sixth place in the AL West with a record of 68–94, 25 games out of first place.

Just two years before, Charlie Finley had sold the Athletics to the Haas family of the Levi Strauss clothing empire, for $12.7 million, some $4.7 million more than Finley had sought before Martin arrived. Billy thought he had earned a bonus for improving the value of the team. Finley disagreed.

With Finley out of the picture, the new owners refused to honor Charlie's commitment to Martin that Billy have sole authority on player moves. As an alternative, and to ensure his security in the job, Martin asked for a long-term contract.

The new owners had their own alternative to Martin's request. The makers of blue jeans gave Martin a pink slip.

Fifteen
BILLY'S BACK

The cover of the 1983 *Yankees Information Guide* depicts a cartoon caricature of a man in a pinstriped uniform face-to-face with a man in a blue American League umpire's uniform. The man in the Yankee uniform wears a mustache and a scowl on his face, anger in his eyes. The index finger of his right hand is pointed at the umpire's nose.

Yes, Billy Martin was back. Eighty-four days after he was let go by the Oakland Athletics, Martin returned for a third time as manager of the New York Yankees, and he would not have Reggie Jackson to kick around anymore. After the 1981 season, Mr. October had attained free agency for a second time and had escaped the Bronx Zoo for the relative peace and serenity of Southern California by signing with the California Angels.

Five managers had been in his seat in the Yankee dugout since Martin last occupied it—Dick Howser, Gene Michael, Bob Lemon, Michael again, and Clyde King, who managed the final 62 games of the 1982 season as the Yankees limped home in fifth place in the American League East, 16 games out of first, with a record of 79–83.

In spring training, George Steinbrenner had vowed his loyalty to Lemon, in his second tour as manager of the Yankees.

"I'm not going to make a change in 1982 unless it's dictated by something other than how the team is doing," Steinbrenner told the media. "I swear on my heart, (Lemon will) be my manager all season."

Lemon lasted all of 14 games. With the Yankees' record at 6–8, Lemon was fired and replaced by Gene Michael, who would be replaced by Clyde King, setting the stage for Billy III.

Why did Martin come back? Why would he put himself once again in the position of taking the heat when things did not go well, being second-guessed, having his job threatened, being dictated to?

The simple answer was that he loved the Yankees, that he relished the challenge, that he had the confidence, and the ego, to turn the team into a winner. He needed to manage a baseball team like a pig needs to wallow in slop.

But why would he work for George Steinbrenner again?

"When George presents it the way he does—'Gee, Billy, I really need you. You have to come back and manage for me. Do me a favor. Help me'—when he says it like that, I can't say no," Martin would say. "I can't turn him down, because he has always been there to help me when I needed something.

"George is a man of many personalities. There's the demanding, hard-driving Boss Steinbrenner; the considerate, charming, and compassionate Steinbrenner; the sensitive, helpful, charity-minded Steinbrenner.

"I think down deep George is a good person who means well, even though he sometimes doesn't go about things properly.

There are times I like George so much I'd fight a horse for him. Then there are other times when I would like to throw him right out of the nearest window.

"George has always been good to me financially *after* he fired me. My problems with him always have come while I was managing his team. That's true not only of me; it's true of anybody who works for him. The reason he is so demanding on people who work for him is that he is demanding of himself. Nobody works harder than George. Nobody puts in more hours than he does.

"There are a lot of good points about him, and there are a lot of bad points about him. There's one good point that I especially like. He wants the Yankees to win. He wants them to be the best, and he gives his whole heart and soul for that. To me, that's the bottom line. In that way, we're alike. We both want the Yankees to win, and that's why I can never get too angry with him for too long. We both have the same end in mind, even if we differ, disagree, and even fight over the means to that end.

"That's why I came back, and that's why I think it's going to be different this time."

How different was it?

After a lukewarm start, the Yankees began heating up in May. They won seven out of nine games, followed that up with six straight wins, climbed over .500, and on June 1, moved into second place in the AL East, a half game behind the Toronto Blue Jays.

Reinvigorated by his return to the Yankees, looking rested and relaxed, Billy Martin was working his managerial magic once more, pushing the Yankees to another championship.

Before the month was out, however, there would be rumors that Martin was about to be fired and replaced by another Yankees idol, Martin's coach and longtime friend Yogi Berra.

Twice Martin was suspended for disputes with umpires, just as was depicted on the *Yankees Information Guide,* a case of life imitating art. But in these disputes, Martin had an ally. George Steinbrenner was fined $50,000 and suspended by Major League Baseball for one week for criticizing the umpires.

It wouldn't be long before Steinbrenner switched sides and flipped on Martin. After reaching their June 1 high, the Yankees lost five out of seven games to California, Seattle, and Cleveland at home and fell back into fifth place, three and a half games out of first as they prepared to take off on a seven-game trip to Milwaukee and Cleveland, with a day off scheduled on June 9, the day before the first game of the trip. Furious with the team's lethargic play in those seven games, Steinbrenner ordered Martin to hold a workout in Milwaukee on the day off.

Martin was of the belief that a day away from the ballpark was a better solution to a midseason slide than a workout for players who may have been getting slightly fatigued. Steinbrenner disagreed. He believed the solution to a slump was to work players harder. Martin and Steinbrenner frequently fought over the issue, as Martin accused Steinbrenner of possessing a "football mentality."

Steinbrenner, Martin said, "never learned to understand the 162-game schedule. He tries to run his baseball team like a football team, but football teams don't play every day. They play once a week, a 16-game schedule. There's a big difference. By its nature, and the short schedule, football is an emotional game. By its nature, and the long, daily grind, baseball is not an emotional game.

"Football players don't pull their socks up every day from the start of spring training in February to the end of the season in October. Because George has never played the game, he doesn't understand that sometimes you get tired just pulling up those socks every day. You get mentally fatigued.

"You have to go through it to understand that. You have to be out there every day to appreciate what it's like, to know what those players go through. He never did it, so it always has been a difficult thing to get across to him.

"George doesn't understand what it takes out of a player to play in all those spring training games. He doesn't understand what two days off can do for a player, mentally and physically. It can seem like a two-week vacation on a desert island. He doesn't understand that sometimes it's better to give a team the day off rather than have them work out, even when they're not playing well. Maybe the reason they're not playing well is that they're tired, physically tired and mentally and emotionally drained by the long season and the traveling and playing every day without a break. He doesn't understand that one day away from baseball can be the best tonic of all."

In the past, Martin never could win that battle, so when Steinbrenner ordered him to call a workout for the day off in Milwaukee, the manager backed down and said, "OK, you're the boss."

Martin told his players there would be a workout in Milwaukee on the day off, but what he told the players, but did not reveal to Steinbrenner, was that the workout was voluntary for players and coaches.

To exacerbate Martin's problems, he had been smitten by a beautiful young woman named Jill Guiver, 30 years his junior, whom he had met when she showed up at a Yankees game with photographer's credentials. Soon Martin and Jill, who would become the fourth Mrs. Billy Martin, were inseparable. Martin even took Jill on road trips, which was both good and bad news. The good news was that, with Jill along, Martin was not as likely to spend nights after games in bars, where he was in danger of getting involved in another altercation.

The bad news was that during games, Martin seemed to be focusing more on Jill and her comfort than he was on what was happening on the field.

In the first game of a series in Milwaukee, while the Yankees were coasting to a 7–1 victory over the Brewers, Martin was carrying on a shouting match with County Stadium security guards over Martin's concerns for Jill's safety in leaving the stadium.

Two days later, a sultry Sunday afternoon, as the Yankees were losing to the Brewers, Jill was spotted sitting next to the Yankee dugout wearing a revealing and provocative halter top and shorts that barely concealed her voluptuous form. And Martin was seen sitting on the top step of the dugout, only inches away from Jill, who from time to time was passing notes to the manager with her toes.

The game was televised back to New York, where a reporter from the *New York Post* witnessed the flirtatious scene between Martin and his girlfriend. The reporter telephoned Steinbrenner at his home in Tampa and told him what was going on. Steinbrenner had also been tipped off by one of the team's coaches that Martin had defied The Boss's order by making the workout on the day off voluntary. To Steinbrenner, this was gross insubordination worthy of dismissal of the manager.

As the Yankees left Milwaukee and flew to Cleveland, heading to the same city were Steinbrenner and Martin's lawyer, Judge Eddie Sapir. Steinbrenner had made up his mind that Martin had to go, and he was prepared to name Yogi Berra to replace him, but he agreed to meet with Martin and Sapir on Monday, June 13.

The three met at a Cleveland pub, and, as he had done in the past, Steinbrenner began having second thoughts about firing his manager. He decided to give Martin a reprieve on the condition that Billy change his ways and begin to instill discipline in his players. But Martin would not get off without Steinbrenner exacting a familiar penalty, the firing of Art Fowler, Martin's longtime pitching coach, friend, ally, confidant, and drinking companion.

Reluctantly, Martin accepted Steinbrenner's terms, but he would harbor resentment toward Steinbrenner for the shabby treatment of Fowler, an innocent pawn in this sordid affair.

In the midst of all the turmoil, Martin Magic popped up in one memorable moment against the Kansas City Royals at Yankee Stadium on July 24. The Yankees started the day in fourth place, but only two games out of first in the squeaky-tight American League East race.

The surging Yankees entered the top of the ninth leading 4–3, and when they retired the first two Royals batters, they were one out away from their ninth victory in 10 games. When U. L. Washington singled to keep the game alive, Martin called on his bullpen stopper Goose Gossage to face the dangerous George Brett, who blasted a Gossage fastball deep into the upper deck in right field to give the Royals a sudden 5–4 lead.

As Brett circled the bases, Martin was out of the dugout, heading toward home plate umpire Tim McClelland.

Earlier in the season, Graig Nettles had mentioned to Martin that he noticed Brett's bat was layered with pine tar from top to bottom, an apparent violation of rule 1.10(b): The bat handle, for not more than 18 inches from its end, may be covered or treated with any material or substance to improve the grip. Any such material or substance which extends past the 18-inch limitation shall cause the bat to be removed from the game.

Martin made note of Nettles' discovery and told Nettles he would not register a complaint right away, but would wait until Brett delivered a damaging hit against the Yankees with the tainted bat. The time was now.

Martin brought his case to McClelland, who laid Brett's bat against the width of home plate (17 inches by rule) and agreed with Martin: The pine tar on the bat did, indeed, extend more than 18 inches from the end. After consulting with his umpiring crew chief, Joe Brinkman, who agreed, McClelland ruled Brett out and the game over, awarding the Yankees a 4–3 victory.

At that point, Brett went berserk, racing wild-eyed out of the Royals dugout in the direction of McClelland, his manager, Dick Howser, right behind him. Brett had to be restrained from attacking McClelland. Howser, somewhat more in control than

Brett, argued his case with McClelland and told the umpire he was protesting the game to American League president Lee MacPhail.

Four days later, MacPhail handed down his ruling, upholding the Royals protest on the grounds that the intent of the rule was to prevent doctoring bats for the purpose of improving "the distance factor or caus[ing] unusual reaction on the baseball."

Citing "the spirit of the rule," MacPhail said it was clear that there was no such intent on Brett's part, and he ordered the game replayed from the point of the home run, the resumption of the game to take place in Yankee Stadium on August 18, an open date for both teams.

Steinbrenner was livid with MacPhail's decision. "It sure tests our faith in our leadership," he said. "If the Yankees lose the American League pennant by one game, I wouldn't want to be Lee MacPhail living in New York. Maybe he should go house hunting in Kansas City."

For that remark, Steinbrenner, who had already been fined $50,000 by MacPhail for criticizing umpires, was assessed a $300,000 fine by Commissioner Bowie Kuhn.

At least Martin and Steinbrenner had found a common ground and reached an accord on something.

"MacPhail not only ruled against the umpires, he ruled against the rules book," Martin said. "The reason the decision went against us was that George and MacPhail had been fighting with each other. And I was right in the middle of the whole thing. It wasn't Billy Martin vs. The Rules; it was Lee MacPhail vs. George Steinbrenner fighting all the time, and Lee let his fight with George overshadow his good thinking and cloud his good judgment.

"There's no question that the rule should have been rewritten, and it was. As it was written, it was a bad rule and an ambiguous one. But that wasn't my fault. I didn't write the rules. The way this rule was written, I was right, and there was no question of that.

"My argument was why make these rules if you're not going to follow them? You tell me to follow every other rule, now there comes one that I follow to the letter, and I'm right, and that one you're going to change?"

As the summer dragged on, it became clear that Martin was losing his grip as well as his ability to rally his team, and Steinbrenner was growing increasingly disenchanted with his manager. After a brief spurt that saw the Yankees move into second place, they began to backslide and slowly fell out of the race in September. Although they would win 91 games, 12 more than the previous season, the Yankees finished in third place, 7 games behind the Orioles.

On December 16, the Yankees announced that Billy Martin would not return as manager in 1984. Like the proverbial cat, Martin had used up three of his lives. Billy III was over, although he would continue with the Yankees as a consultant and scout. His successor as manager, as had been forecast six months earlier, would be Yogi Berra.

The perception around baseball for years was that Yogi Berra was the luckiest man on earth. Whatever he touched turned to gold. He could fall into a manhole and come up with a $1,000 bill.

He bought a bowling alley and made a handsome profit by selling it during the bowling boom in the 1950s. A year later, when the boom bottomed out, he bought the alley back for half as much as he received when he sold it.

He invested money in and contributed his name to a small soft drink company, and two decades later he became a vice president of Yoo-hoo.

He became manager of the Yankees in 1964 and won the American League pennant in his first season.

He was named manager of the New York Mets in 1972 after Gil Hodges died of a heart attack and a year later led them to their second National League pennant.

"Yogi is one of those Christmas Eve guys," Berra's boyhood pal Joe Garagiola once said. "There are people like that. There are people who are December 17th guys or October 19th guys. Me, I'm an April 10th guy. And there are people who are Christmas Eve guys. Every day in their lives is Christmas Eve. Stan Musial always was a Christmas Eve guy. So is Yogi."

Yogi Berra lucky? Not here, not now. He would manage a team owned by George Steinbrenner, and he would do it in 1984, when the Detroit Tigers would win 35 of their first 40 games and run away with the American League East title, leaving Berra, the Yankees, and everybody else in their dust.

The Yankees got off to a slow start under Berra, and then things got worse. By May 1, they were in seventh place, 11½ games out of first. By July 1, they were 33–42 and had fallen 21 games behind the Tigers, and Berra was feeling Steinbrenner's wrath. To make his displeasure known, Steinbrenner did what he often did: He called a meeting.

Steinbrenner summoned Berra and his coaches to his office in Yankee Stadium and began the meeting with a tirade aimed mostly at his manager. Steinbrenner ranted as Berra listened wordlessly, staring at the floor in front of him and clenching his fists in an effort to control himself. Finally, Berra could take it no longer. He rose from his seat, fired a pack of cigarettes toward Steinbrenner, and went off on an expletive-filled vocal rampage at Steinbrenner. He then stormed out of the room.

Was this the end of Berra as manager of the Yankees? Everyone in the room expected nothing less, but Steinbrenner watched Berra leave and calmly said, "I guess the pressure of losing is getting to him."

Not only was Berra not fired on the spot, his outburst seemed to get Steinbrenner off his back. What is it they say about bullies? They rule by intimidation and recoil at confrontation.

The previous year, Goose Gossage had stood up to Steinbrenner and also escaped unscathed. It was in August of a dismal season, but Gossage had saved both games of a doubleheader against the Royals, and reporters, looking for something positive to write about in this awful season, flocked to Gossage's locker.

Normally the most cordial, cooperative, and mild-mannered of men (off the field, not on), Gossage, no doubt frustrated by the wasted season, let loose an expletive-laden harangue. In the middle of his tirade, Gossage addressed the radio reporters carrying their tape recorders and stormed, "You can turn it on and take it upstairs to the fat man, OK?"

When Steinbrenner was told of Gossage's remarks, he reacted in uncharacteristic fashion. Instead of expressing anger at the pitcher's insubordination, as he had done on other occasions with other insults, Steinbrenner meekly responded, "Tell Goose I've been on a diet and I've lost 11 pounds since June."

Although Berra survived his tirade, nobody expected him to return the following season. Steinbrenner had already changed managers 10 times in 10 years, so making it 11 was not going to cause much of a ripple. But in the second half, Berra led the Yankees to the major leagues' best record, 51–29, which earned him one more year as manager of the Yankees.

On the day before the Yankees were to begin 1985 spring training, Steinbrenner held another meeting in Fort Lauderdale with Berra and his coaches. This time, he emerged from the meeting and announced: "Yogi Berra will be the manager for the whole year. A bad start will not affect Yogi's status."

A bad start is exactly what Steinbrenner got, the Yankees opening the season in Boston and losing the first two games to the Red Sox by the lopsided scores of 9–2 and 14–5, with Steinbrenner in attendance at Fenway Park.

Sensing another Steinbrenner blowup, reporters descended on the owner after the second game and were told that the next day's game, the third game of the season, was "crucial." It was, by all accounts, the earliest crucial game in baseball history.

The Yankees lost that "crucial" game, too, and reporters went on "Yogi Watch." But the Yankees rebounded to win five of their next six games before going into another slide, three straight losses to Cleveland and Boston, a win over the Red Sox, then two straight losses at the start of a six-game trip to Chicago and Texas.

After the second loss in Chicago, on Saturday, April 27, general manager Clyde King, traveling with the team, received a call from Steinbrenner, who told King that he had decided to make a change after the next day's game. Berra, whom Steinbrenner said would be the Yankees manager "for the whole year," would be relieved of his duties. After 16 games!

Berra's replacement, Steinbrenner said, would be . . . drum roll here, a blare of trumpets, and try not to look surprised . . . Billy Martin.

Sixteen

"NOW PITCHING, ED WHITSON . . . CATCHING, BILLY MARTIN"

When they learned there would be a Billy IV, Billy Martin's legion of fans was thrilled. Others were not, Yankees players included.

Rumors had been flying for several days, so when the Yankees lost the first two games of their series with the White Sox in Chicago on April 27, 1985, and general manager Clyde King entered the clubhouse, went straight to manager Yogi Berra's office, and closed the door, the players knew what was coming.

Soon the word circulated around the clubhouse. Berra was out as manager, and Billy Martin was in. There was open revolt among the players, partly because of their affection for Berra, partly because of how unfair it was that he would be let go after only 16 games, and partly because they wanted no part of playing for Martin.

Don Baylor kicked over a trash container. Don Mattingly escaped to the trainers' room and tossed objects against the wall. Copies of the release announcing the change in managers were handed out to players, most of whom tore them up or crumpled them and tossed them aside.

So beloved was Berra that, to a man, each Yankee walked into the manager's office, gave Yogi a hug or shook his hand, and wished him well. Some players were in tears.

Not surprising, the player who took the news hardest was Dale Berra, Yogi's son, who had come to the Yankees in a trade with the Pirates during the winter.

"You have your career ahead of you," Yogi told Dale. "I've already had mine. Billy Martin's a good man. You've known him since you were a kid. Just play hard for him, that's all he asks. Don't worry about me. I'll be watching what you do."

Yogi, true to form, was taking his firing like a man.

"It's his [Steinbrenner's] team," he told the writers. "He can do with it what he wants. It was going to happen sooner or later, so we might as well get it over now."

As for watching what his son, Dale, was doing, it was going to have to be on television. Yogi was so hurt, felt so betrayed by getting fired only 16 games into the season, and so angry that Steinbrenner didn't have the courage to confront him face-to-face, he vowed never to return to Yankee Stadium "as long as he's there."

He never said who "he" was. Nobody had to ask.

(Berra would boycott Yankee Stadium and refuse to go there for 14 years, until Steinbrenner, hat in hand, went to the Yogi Berra Museum in Montclair, New Jersey, and personally extended an olive branch to the Hall of Fame catcher, begged him to return to the Yankees family, and told Yogi he wanted to honor him with a Yogi Berra Day.)

The Yankees left Chicago without Berra and flew by charter to Texas. When they arrived at the Arlington Hilton, Martin was waiting for them with his lawyer, Judge Eddie Sapir. Writers traveling with the team were invited by Sapir to Martin's suite to meet with Billy.

"This time it's going to be different," Sapir said of Martin's return for Billy IV, by now a familiar refrain. "Billy and George really understand each other now."

"That's right," Martin jumped in. "George and I have talked a lot, and we have an understanding. The main thing is we both want to win."

Had Yogi Berra been in attendance in Martin's suite, he might have characterized the onset of Billy IV as "déjà vu all over again."

When he addressed the team, Martin pulled no punches.

"I didn't get Yogi fired," he told his players, "you did. You love Yogi so much? You should have played for him. If you did, he'd still be here."

As he had done so often in the past, in so many places, Martin had an almost immediate positive impact on the team. After losing the first two games of his return, Martin got the Yankees rolling. They won four straight games, lost two, won two, lost one, and then ran off a six-game winning streak. In three weeks, Martin had pushed, prodded, and manipulated the Yankees from seventh place, six games out of first, to fourth place, two and a half games behind.

Slowly, the Yankees moved up in the standings. They advanced to second place on July 13 but were unable to gain ground on the first-place Toronto Blue Jays. By the first week of August the Yankees, still in second place, had fallen nine and a half games behind, their hopes of catching the Blue Jays growing dimmer by the day.

But Martin and the Yankees had another run left in them. They put together two seven-game winning streaks, wrapped around a loss. With 14 victories in 15 games and 17 of 19, they moved 3 games behind Toronto. On August 31, the Yankees beat the Angels to launch an 11-game winning streak, but they could shave only a game and a half off the Blue Jays lead and still trailed by a game and a half. Still, the Yankees were charging hard, their hopes of catching the Blue Jays soaring.

On September 12, the Yankees were two and a half games behind but confident they would wipe out that deficit in a head-to-head four-game series with the Blue Jays at Yankee Stadium. When they won the first game of the series, 7–6, the Yankees were thinking sweep, which would put them in first place. Three out of four would leave them a half game behind with 20 games to play and momentum on their side.

But as had happened so often in the past, in so many places, Martin could not stand prosperity. The Yankees lost the next three games to Toronto and fell four and a half games back. Soon Martin would be embroiled in more controversy and make some bizarre managerial decisions, his history for self-destruction surfacing once more to threaten his job.

On September 16, the Yankees faced the Cleveland Indians in a make-up game caused by an earlier rainout. Leading 5–3 going to the ninth inning, Martin stayed with pitcher Brian Fisher, who had won only four games, rather than bring in his closer, Dave Righetti, who would finish the season with 12 wins and 29 saves. Martin never made a move to his bullpen while the Indians pounded Fisher for six runs and Righetti stood in the bullpen, hands on his hips.

"When I went out to see Brian Fisher," Martin explained, "I knew what I wanted to hear. I wanted him to stay in, but I wanted him to tell me. You can't ask the catcher how he thinks the pitcher is throwing. At least you can't ask him in front of the pitcher. The catcher might lie to spare the pitcher's feelings. And 95 times out of 100, if you ask the pitcher if he's tired, he's going to say no because he wants to stay in there.

"It didn't surprise me that Fisher said he was OK. If he was wishy-washy about it, I would have yanked him. But he was anything but wishy-washy. I asked him if he wanted to come out, and he said, 'Oh, please, Billy, let me stay in.' That was exactly what I expected to hear and exactly what I wanted to hear."

For all his accepted genius as a manager, Martin had acquired a reputation as someone who ruined pitchers, overused them, abused them, and ultimately destroyed them.

Was the reputation deserved? To some extent it was. Many of his pitchers eventually broke down, and the reason given by Martin's detractors was overuse. What was likely more factual was that Martin was a product of his time, an era when managers paid no heed to pitch counts, and pitchers wanted to finish what they started.

The record supports Martin as a manager who got more, not less, out of his pitchers.

Under Martin's watch, Ron Guidry won 20 games three times, Mickey Lolich twice, Joe Coleman twice, and Jim Perry, Dave Boswell, Ferguson Jenkins, Mike Norris, and Ed Figueroa once. None of them won 20 games under any other manager except Hall of Famer Jenkins and Guidry and Figueroa, who each won 20 in 1978, when Martin was replaced in midseason by Bob Lemon.

"I had a great time with Billy, mainly because I loved to pitch," said Figueroa, who, in 1978, became the first native-born Puerto Rican to win 20 games. "I told him I want to pitch every fourth day. He knew I didn't want to miss any starts, and I wanted to stay in there to win games. He was great to me. He treated me pretty good."

Suddenly five games out of first and with time running out, the Yankees embarked on a trip that would take them to Detroit for three games and then to Baltimore for three more. In Detroit, the Yankees were bombed in the first game by the Tigers, 9–1, as Martin allowed Ron Guidry to absorb a five home run onslaught.

The next night, Martin made a move that left observers thinking he had completely taken leave of his senses. With the score tied 2–2, in the sixth, runners on first and third, two outs and left-handed hitting Mike Pagliarulo coming to bat against left-hander Mickey Mahler, Martin had a brainstorm . . . or brain cramp. Billy had watched Pagliarulo look helpless against Mahler in his first two at bats, striking out both times. He also had seen Pagliarulo take batting practice batting right-handed and regularly hit balls to the warning track.

Unfortunately, batting practice pitching is not like the pitching in a game, and Pagliarulo had never batted right-handed in a game. Nevertheless, Martin told hitting coach Lou Piniella to instruct Pagliarulo to hit right-handed against Mahler. At first, Pagliarulo thought Piniella was joking. When he was convinced Piniella was serious, Pagliarulo did as he was told and took his place in the right-handed hitter's batter's box. It was a surprise to Mahler, catcher Bob Melvin, Tigers manager Sparky Anderson, the Tigers players, the Yankees players, the writers and broadcasters, the vendors, and the 20,318 fans in Tiger Stadium. But nobody was surprised when Pagliarulo looked at a third strike to end the rally.

The Yankees lost the third game of the series and went on to Baltimore on a seven-game losing streak, five and a half games out of first and all but eliminated from contention. Martin had told the writers that to open the Orioles series, he was skipping Ed Whitson, whose turn it was, because, according to the manager, "Whitson has a sore arm."

Told by the writers that the manager said he had a "sore arm," Whitson began laughing uproariously.

The Yankees lost the first game of the series, extending their slide to eight straight, their season rapidly slipping out of control. So, it seemed, was Martin. During a key situation in the 4–2 loss, he inadvertently gave the sign for a pitchout in the sixth inning, with the score tied 2–2, a runner on first, and a 2–0 count on the batter. The batter eventually walked and both runners scored to give the Orioles a lead they would not relinquish.

With the game over, Martin, as was his custom, headed directly to the hotel bar, where he got into an altercation with a fan who accosted Martin for insulting the fan's wife.

"You told my wife she has a pot belly," the fan said.

"I did not," Martin insisted. He pointed to another woman at the bar and said, "I said that woman has a fat ass."

There was some poking and pushing until several Yankees interceded, separating Martin and the fan.

"We'll take this outside," Martin roared, but when he went into the lobby, the fan was nowhere to be found, and the whole thing ended without further incident. The cessation of hostilities would last less than 24 hours.

The next night, after the Yankees had finally put an end to their losing streak with a 5–2 win over the Orioles, Martin again went to the bar, where he met up with Dale Berra and Berra's wife. Seated at a table no farther away than the distance from home plate to first base was pitcher Ed Whitson and a group of friends, their table overrun with beer bottles. A few minutes later, Martin could be seen entangled with Whitson, the two grabbing at each other.

There were no witnesses to how and what had started the tussle. Martin later would say he had come to the aid of his pitcher, who was being bothered by some fans. Told of Martin's explanation, Whitson said such a thing never happened.

What started the ruckus remained a mystery, but its result was much more overt. Soon Martin and Whitson were rolling on the floor, while several Yankees and Whitson's friends tried vainly to act as peacemakers.

"That guy's crazy," Martin shouted. "I was just trying to help him. What's the matter with him? Can't he hold his liquor?"

The more Martin yelled, the more Whitson yelled back, screaming and cursing the manager. And the more Whitson yelled back, the more enraged Martin became. He advanced at the pitcher, and the two wound up in the hotel lobby, where Martin got close enough to the pitcher for Whitson to kick Martin in the groin with his cowboy-booted right foot.

Doubled over in pain, Martin yelled, "Okay, now I'm going to kill you. Now you did it."

Before Martin could make good on his threat, Whitson was hustled out of the lobby by his friends and the Yankees peacemakers. In so doing, Dale Berra took a punch to the mouth from

Whitson that resulted in a split lip. Suddenly Martin broke loose from those who were restraining him and charged Whitson, tackling him onto the pavement in front of the hotel entrance. The hotel's security men had arrived, and they quickly broke the two combatants apart. Martin had a bloody nose and was holding his right arm.

By this time, the police had arrived, and they succeeded in restoring peace . . . but only temporarily. Martin returned to the bar, but after a few minutes, still fuming, he stormed out, announcing he was going to find Whitson. He stopped at the front desk to get the pitcher's room number and headed up in pursuit of Whitson.

As luck would have it, at the moment Martin was getting off the elevator on Whitson's floor, Whitson was getting off the elevator next to Martin's. They began shouting at each other, but hotel security and Whitson's friends kept them apart and prevented further mayhem.

The next day, Martin arrived at the stadium with his arm in a cast. He had sustained a fracture in the melee. Whitson was nowhere to be found; General Manager Clyde King had sent him home. Informed of the scuffle, George Steinbrenner ordered Assistant General Manager Woody Woodward to Baltimore to investigate the incident and report back to him.

Miraculously, the Battle of Baltimore seemed to energize the Yankees, who took the third game of the three-game series against the Orioles, lost to Detroit, then ran off eight wins in their next nine games. The Yankees were still alive in the race, three games behind the Blue Jays with three games remaining in Toronto. The Yankees were happy to have their fate in their hands. A sweep of the three-game series by the Yankees would leave them and the

Blue Jays with identical records at the end of the season. More important, a sweep would give the Yankees a 7–6 edge against the Blue Jays in their season series, and, as such, the Yankees would be awarded the division championship.

Hopes soared for the Yankees when they scored two runs in the top of the ninth in the first game of the series, came from behind, and beat the Jays, 4–3.

But the next day, Doyle Alexander stifled Yankee bats on five hits for a complete-game 5–1 victory that clinched the division title for Toronto. The Yankees would end the season with a close-but-no-cigar 8–0 win over the Jays.

The consensus was that Martin had done a masterful job of managing that year. He won 97 games, 10 more than the Yankees had won the previous season, and he brought them back into contention from a deficit of 7 games with 12 games to play. Even George Steinbrenner had to agree.

But was it enough to compensate for the several bizarre moves Martin had made and for the barroom brawls?

The answer came on October 27, when the Yankees announced that Martin had been fired (again) and that hitting instructor Lou Piniella would take over as manager of the team in 1986.

Seventeen
PROUDEST YANKEE

Lou Piniella had reasons to believe things would be different for him as manager of the Yankees, a belief he based on his unique relationship with The Boss. Piniella knew he enjoyed the privilege of being a favorite of George Steinbrenner. He was one of the few players/employees who could banter with Steinbrenner with a well-honed needle and survive, like the time at a meeting when Steinbrenner was ranting over leaks to the press from Yankees employees unknown. To seal the leaks, Steinbrenner ordered lie detector tests be taken by everyone in the organization.

"I'll take one as long as you take one, George," Piniella said.

The Piniellas and Steinbrenners were both residents of Tampa, and they occasionally socialized. Steinbrenner often said he thought of Piniella as a son, so Piniella reasoned he would not have to endure the same second-guessing, the same meddling, the same demands other managers had.

What Piniella discovered to his chagrin was that the only thing different was the way one is perceived once he becomes Steinbrenner's manager. Then he is fair game for the second-guessing, the meddling, and the demands. When you manage for George Steinbrenner, you are in his crosshairs no matter who you are.

Not at first. Piniella was even able to make light of a potentially volatile situation when Steinbrenner second-guessed Piniella's lineup for a spring training game. Instead of lashing out at The Boss, as Billy Martin would have done, Piniella had an idea. He suggested that Steinbrenner manage the following day's game against the Orioles. Steinbrenner would make out the starting lineup and take a seat next to the Yankee dugout. From there, he could run the game, flashing signs for the steal, the bunt, the hit-and-run, to third base coach Gene Michael, who would relay them to the players.

Steinbrenner agreed, at first. Later, he reconsidered.

"Oh, no you don't," he told Piniella. "You're not going to trick me that easy. You're the manager. You do the managing. I'm the owner. I'll do the second-guessing. That's the way it's supposed to be."

The first serious disagreement between Steinbrenner and Piniella came at a meeting of The Boss, the manager, coaches, and front office personnel to determine final cuts prior to the start of the season. At issue was what to do with 45-year-old knuckleball pitcher Phil Niekro, a Hall of Famer-in-waiting who had won 16 games for the Yankees in each of the previous two seasons. To Piniella and his coaches, Niekro, despite his advanced age, was still an effective pitcher worth keeping. Steinbrenner thought otherwise, and his was the vote that counted.

"Why are you even bothering to ask our opinion?" Piniella stormed. "You know what you're going to do anyway."

Reluctantly, Piniella had the unpleasant task of telling Niekro, a player with whom he had formed a special relationship, that he was being released.

Except for the Niekro incident, the 1986 season, Piniella's first as manager, passed relatively free of the usual turmoil that had surrounded the Yankees in the Billy Martin years. Steinbrenner seemed to be willing to keep Piniella on a long leash and suffer the growing pains of a first-year manager, especially after the Yankees got off to a good start and were in first place in the middle of May.

As manager, Piniella experienced more than a little discomfort when Billy Martin, still under contract to the Yankees as a special consultant to the principal owner, began showing up in the owner's box (the very thing Martin had resented in 1976 when Dick Williams, like Martin, was seen in Steinbrenner's box). Martin had Steinbrenner's ear and was said to be openly critical of some of Piniella's moves, a clear indication that Billy still had not accepted being on the outside looking in and still aspired to manage the team.

When he relieved Billy Martin as manager after the 1985 season, George Steinbrenner kept him on the payroll under the amorphous title of "special advisory staff." It meant Martin would be available as a consultant, troubleshooter, scout, and any other role Steinbrenner could find to keep Billy occupied and out of trouble, including that of television analyst on Yankee games. He was a commentator on the pre- and postgame and for two innings during the game, which Martin found unfulfilling.

"I might sit there for two innings, and nothing important happens," he complained. "The key play of the game might come up when I'm not on the air, and I don't get to comment on it. I think that's a waste of what I can contribute. I'd like to do more, but that's not up to me."

While his on-air work was never going to make listeners forget Mel Allen, Martin received good grades for his content. His boss, Don Carney, producer of Yankee telecasts for WPIX-TV, gave him a thumbs-up. In the past, pleasing his boss had often been a problem for Martin, but some bosses are harder to please than others.

"The mail has been very favorable," Carney said. "In this business, most of the mail you get is negative. The fact that the majority of the mail on Billy is positive has to weigh very heavily in his favor. The thing most people comment on is how much he has improved, and I certainly agree with that."

Some of his critics suggested that Martin was using his TV gig to campaign for a higher position, like managing the Yankees one more time. They accused him of second-guessing and backstabbing his successor as manager, Lou Piniella.

"I know of no case where he has second-guessed me," Piniella said. "I'm sure I would have heard about it if he did. Look, he has to say what he feels and what he sees. I have no problem with that. And I have no problem with anything he has said. I consider Billy a friend. I love the guy. He's a good man."

Early in the season, when the Bombers' pitching was in shambles, Martin was asked on air if he had any solutions.

"Maybe the time has come to think about putting Dave Righetti back in the starting rotation," he responded.

"That's not a second-guess," said Piniella. "That's an opinion, and he's entitled to it."

If anything, Piniella said, Martin was supportive of him. In one telecast, he went out of his way to praise the job Piniella was doing in patching together a pitching staff depleted by injuries.

"One thing people don't realize," Martin said, "is that Lou has held the club together. For a rookie manager, that's not an easy thing to do. He's doing it like a veteran manager. He's done an amazing job, and not enough people have written about it."

"I heard about that," Piniella said. "That was nice of him."

Piniella even pointed out that he had taken advantage of Martin's friendship and his expertise and experience by getting together with his predecessor on road trips.

"The guy's the best baseball man around," Piniella said. "I'm a secure person. Having a man like that around and not taking advantage of his expertise is foolish. I sat with him, and I ran ideas through him. We talked about the team and about managing in general. It was great therapy for me. The guy's great."

"I never made any suggestions," Martin said. "I wouldn't do that. Mostly, I listened to him, and I might tell him what I would do in a similar situation. Then I said, 'But you're the manager, you do things the way you want to do them.'

"One thing I insist on with the other announcers is not to ask me, 'What would you do if you were the manager?' That's not fair. I'm not the manager. I'm not down there like Lou is. You have to be in the pits to know the pulse of the team."

What he was unable to achieve as a manager, Martin achieved as a commentator: approval from Steinbrenner.

"The sucker knows his baseball," The Boss lauded. "He predicts things one day, and the next day they happen. I'm pleased with what he's done. I don't know of any case where he's second-guessed Lou. But if he wants to, that's fine. If he has an opinion, he should express it. That's part of the game. I told Billy not to be afraid to express his opinions. He second-guessed the front office on some player move. That's OK. Nobody in this organization, from the lowest player to the top guy, should be free of criticism, as long as it's fair."

In addition to keeping Martin on the payroll after firing him, Steinbrenner promised there would be a Billy Martin Day at Yankee Stadium. Billy's uniform No. 1 would be permanently retired, and his plaque would be added to Monument Park, alongside the other Yankee legends—Babe Ruth, Lou Gehrig, Joe DiMaggio, his pals Mickey Mantle and Whitey Ford, and his mentor, Casey Stengel.

It was a typical maneuver for Steinbrenner: ruthless and demanding when he was your boss; compassionate, generous, and guilt-ridden after he has fired you. He did it with Bob Lemon. He did it with Dick Howser. And now he was doing it with Billy Martin.

Billy Martin Day was held on August 10, 1986. Mantle, Ford, and Phil Rizzuto were there, as were many of Martin's other former teammates. Joe DiMaggio and Bobby Richardson sent telegrams. Ron Guidry, representing all the Yankees Martin had managed, presented him with a "No. 1" diamond-and-gold pendant.

When all the dignitaries, and Martin's friends, family, and

former teammates, had been assembled at home plate, Martin's 86-year-old mother, Joan, was introduced. Three months earlier, she had fallen and broken her hip, but she was brought out in a wheelchair. She wore a Yankee pinstriped dress made especially for the occasion and a Yankee cap.

They wheeled her to Martin's side, and as Billy bent over to kiss her, she looked up at him and said, "I look pretty good for an old broad, don't I, Billy?"

The crowd of 40,198 cheered wildly when it was announced that Martin's No. 1 was to be retired, then his plaque was revealed. Announcer Bill White, acting as master of ceremonies, read the inscription:

ALFRED MANUEL "BILLY" MARTIN
CASEY'S BOY

A YANKEE FOREVER. A MAN WHO KNEW
ONLY ONE WAY TO PLAY—TO WIN. AS A
PLAYER FOR CASEY STENGEL, HE
THRIVED ON PRESSURE, DELIVERING
THE KEY PLAY OR HIT. MVP OF THE 1953
WORLD SERIES, SETTING RECORD FOR
MOST HITS IN SIX-GAME SERIES WITH 12.
LATER AS MANAGER HE BECAME ONE
OF THE GREATEST YANKEE MANAGERS.

ERECTED BY
NEW YORK YANKEES
AUGUST 10, 1986

Now, it was Martin's turn to speak, and in a voice heavy with emotion, he told the cheering crowd, "The four most important things in my life have been my family, God, my friends, and being a Yankee. I want to thank all the coaches who helped me in the past; the players who made it possible; and you fans, who are the best in the world, who stuck behind me. I may not have been the greatest Yankee who ever put on the uniform, but I am the proudest."

After the game, there was a reception and dinner at the Sheraton Heights Hotel in Hasbrouck Heights, New Jersey. Mantle and Ford were there. So were Art Fowler and Clete Boyer, Joe Collins and Charlie Silvera, Lee MacPhail, Lou Piniella, and several current Yankees: Guidry, Joe Niekro, Brian Fisher, Dave Righetti, and Tommy John.

Jimmy Piersall, with whom Martin had once fought under the stands, was there. So were Walt Dropo, who was Martin's teammate in Cincinnati; Jackie Moore, who coached for Martin in Oakland; Thurman Munson's widow, Diana; and American League umpire Ken Kaiser. Actor Tom Selleck sent a message delivered by Martin's friend, comedian Tom Dreesen, and so, too, did Frank Sinatra, who said, "I'm the only man in your lifetime who has been in more saloon fights than you. Billy, you know I love you and have for many, many years."

Members of the New York City Police Department came bearing a gift. They knew what few people knew, that Martin had a passionate interest in the Civil War and was an avid reader of the subject. Their gift was an original photograph of General Philip Sheridan.

"Dad read a lot," Billy Martin Jr. remembered. "He always seemed to be reading some book. I think he read himself to sleep. His main interests were the American Indian and the Civil War.

"He didn't talk much publicly about his interest in the Civil War, but the editor of *Blue and Gray* magazine told me that Dad told him he sympathized with the South, that they were forced into doing things they didn't want to do and that Dad admired General Robert E. Lee. He thought he was a great general. I think he related to Lee as a leader of men; that he felt a general was a lot like the manager of a baseball team in that respect.

"I remember Dad telling me that early in the war, they would take Sundays off. They would lay down their arms, and they would play baseball games. It would be the North against the South, and I remember Dad saying, 'Can you imagine how hard those guys were sliding into second base?'"

When Martin got up to talk, he said, "No question, this is the greatest day of my life.

"What is Billy Martin?" he asked. "It's you. You are what it's all about, my friends, my family. People came here from all over the United States. That makes me proud.

"I came from Berkeley, and people said I was too small to play in the big leagues. They said I couldn't adjust to the big city. I've been up and down, and what it boils down to is that the good Lord has taken care of me.

"How do you say thanks? There's no real way. If you have a child that wants to be a major leaguer, God can't give you any more than that. God bless you. I really love you all."

As the summer dragged on, Piniella's Yankees began to seek their level and slide in the standings. On September 10, they reached their low point, 11½ games out of first, and Steinbrenner was heard to say that it had been a mistake turning his team over to someone with no previous managing experience.

A late run in which the Yankees won seven of their final eight games, including a four-game sweep in Boston, left the Yankees with 90 wins, in second place in the American League East, five and a half games out of first, and saved Piniella's job.

If 1986 had been Piniella's "honeymoon" season as manager, 1987 would be his season to prove he deserved to remain on the job. And it wasn't long before Piniella realized the honeymoon was over, his grace period terminated.

The first sign of trouble came in August. The Yankees reached the all-star break in first place by three games with a record of 55–34, but a rash of injuries, especially to his pitching staff, slowed the Yankees and doomed Piniella. The team went on a trip to Cleveland, Detroit, and Kansas City, lost 8 out of 10 games, and fell out of first place. To make matters worse, Steinbrenner, growing increasingly irritable, sent word to Piniella through the team's public relations director to be in his hotel room and available for a 2:00 p.m. telephone call from The Boss.

When Steinbrenner called and his manager failed to answer, the owner became enraged, charging Piniella with gross insubordination. Rumors began surfacing that Piniella's days as manager of the Yankees were numbered.

In an attempt to prolong the inevitable, Piniella met with Steinbrenner on August 28 to clear the air over the missed phone call and to rekindle his relationship with The Boss. By then, however, the Yankees were in a slide, having dropped into third place, four and a half games out of first.

As he often did in face-to-face confrontations, Steinbrenner backed off and gave Piniella a pass. Piniella, who had built up equity with Steinbrenner as a player on three championship teams, and as a friend and a loyal employee, had dodged a bullet, temporarily at least.

But while he seemed to accept Piniella's explanation for missing his phone call, Steinbrenner never gave his manager a vote of confidence, which some considered an ominous sign for Piniella's future as manager.

"After the season, we'll evaluate the job he did," Steinbrenner said. "Lou knows he will be judged by the bottom line, and injuries are no excuse."

At the same time, Steinbrenner challenged Piniella to rally his troops and right the sinking ship. But Piniella couldn't stop the free fall that saw the Yankees plummet to fourth place, 10½ games out of first on September 24. Piniella could see the handwriting on the wall, and he vowed that if the ax fell . . . *when* the ax fell . . . he would never work for Steinbrenner again.

The end came on October 19, 15 days after the Yankees completed their season with a record of 89–73, in fourth place, nine games behind the Tigers. The Yankees announced that Piniella would not be retained as manager in 1988, but he *would* return. He was being moved up into the front office as general manager with a three-year contract.

Piniella rationalized his change of heart by saying that he accepted Steinbrenner's offer because the three-year contract gave him security for his family and because his wife and children enjoyed living in nearby New Jersey and didn't want to leave.

While naming Piniella general manager, the Yankees also revealed the name of his successor as manager. It would be none other than Billy Martin, back in the Yankee dugout, managing for George Steinbrenner for a fifth time.

Eighteen
VODKA AND OLD LACE

His many fans were thrilled that they had Billy Martin and his fire back managing the Yankees one more time. His closest friends thought Martin was mad. He had endured four tours as Yankees manager and had been fired four times. Couldn't he see that a fifth time would bring only more suffering and more pain?

"Billy never worried about losing his job," said Judge Eddie Sapir. "I worried more about him losing a job than he did. He would always tell me, 'It's OK,' and I said, 'It's not OK. You've got this job, you love this job.' But deep down, Billy was going to be Billy. If he lost the job, well, he lost the job.

"In 1978, after Billy resigned from the Yankees, Gabe Paul, who had left the Yankees and was running the Cleveland Indians, came down to New Orleans to see me.

"'We don't have any attendance,' Gabe said. He wanted to structure a really lucrative contract based on attendance clauses and with a whole bunch of other very attractive things. At the time, Billy was under contract to the Yankees, but if you put the Indians offer and what the Yankees were paying him side by side, as far as monetary value, the Cleveland thing was the one to accept. But Billy didn't do that."

In August 1986, while Martin was at liberty, the Chicago White Sox had decided to replace Tony LaRussa, in his ninth season as Sox manager. Ken "Hawk" Harrelson, the White Sox general manager at the time, called Martin to inquire if he was interested in the job. Martin, in turn, called Sapir.

"Billy asked me to go to Chicago to meet with Harrelson and the White Sox owners, Jerry Reinsdorf and Eddie Einhorn.

"'What do you want me to tell them?' I said.

"He said, 'Tell them I said Tony LaRussa is a great manager and they'd be making a big mistake if they fired him.'

"He could have had the White Sox job, but if Billy thought he had an opportunity with the Yankees, none of the other opportunities would have worked. I always said if Billy died and they buried him in Yankee Stadium, he'd have a smile on his face. I don't think anybody, *anybody*, could love the Yankees more than Billy Martin."

If hiring Billy Martin as his manager for the fifth time was George Steinbrenner's way of looking for a quick fix for his Yankees, that's exactly what he got. Billy V started spectacularly, the Yankees winning their first 5 games and 9 of their first 10.

This was Billy Martin at his best, back where he believed he belonged, managing a baseball team; not just *any* baseball team, but the team he loved.

It was typical Billy, doing what he had done so often, coming in and taking over, putting his imprint on a team, improving them immediately. It was inevitable. Also inevitable was Billy being Billy, looking for trouble, finding it, and self-destructing.

On May 2, the Yankees began a seven-game trip. They swept a two-game series in Chicago, then swept a two-game series in Kansas City. The Yankees had a record of 20–8 and a two and a half game lead in the American League East, and Martin was eagerly looking forward to the next stop, a three-game series against the Texas Rangers in Arlington. There he would meet up with his old pal Mickey Mantle and with his son, Billy Joe.

The Yankees lost the first game of the series, 7–6, but Martin made note of how his team battled, fighting back from a 7–1 deficit to score five runs in the top of the ninth. The rally fell short, but Martin took pride in the fact that his team refused to quit.

When the game was over, Martin, as usual, headed straight for the bar at the Arlington Hilton, where he met up with Mantle, Mantle's son, Danny, and Yankees coach Mike Ferraro. After a few drinks, the group decided to move the party to Lace, a nearby topless nightclub.

What transpired next is unclear. What is known is that the Mantles and Ferraro decided to call it a night and left Martin alone at the club. At some point, Martin went into the men's room, where he proceeded to get involved in a skirmish with another patron. Soon a club bouncer and another customer arrived to act as peacemakers, grabbed Martin, and led him out of the men's room.

When Martin loudly objected to their interference, he was led to a rear door and tossed out of the club. In so doing, Martin hit his head on a stucco wall and suffered cuts on his ear and the side of his head. (Martin's version was that the bouncer sucker punched him, but police reports made no mention of a punch.)

A bloody mess, Martin climbed into a taxi and headed back to the hotel. There is no record of how many times Martin avoided detection of his late-night dalliances by hopping a cab and returning to his hotel. This time, however, he was not so fortunate, the victim of bad timing.

When he arrived at the Arlington Hilton in the wee hours, there were dozens of witnesses waiting on the front lawn of the hotel. The hotel's fire alarm had gone off, causing the guests, Steinbrenner included, to be evacuated.

Seeing the condition of his manager, Steinbrenner was horrified. Ordinarily, he might have fired Martin on the spot for this latest episode. But the Yankees had a record of 20–9 and were in first place, so Steinbrenner issued a statement defending his beleaguered manager. Privately, he put Martin on a short leash.

"I felt responsible for the Lace incident because I wasn't there," said Billy Martin Jr., who, at the time, was a student at Texas Tech University in Lubbock, some 250 miles from Arlington. He was supposed to meet up with his father that night, but he had just finished his final exams and rather than make the five-hour drive to Arlington, decided to get a night's sleep and set out fresh the next morning.

"If I had been there," said Billy Joe, "it never would have happened. I would have gotten him out of the club and back to the hotel before any of that. Dad never got into trouble when I was around."

The Yankees lost all three games in Texas, but won 5 of their next 6 and 11 of 14, including 5 in a row, which left them in first place. Martin seemed to have dodged another bullet . . . but only temporarily.

On May 30, the Yankees lost a 3–2, 14-inning heartbreaker to the Athletics in Oakland. Martin had been ejected in the third inning when umpire Dale Scott ruled a line drive to shortstop Bobby Meacham was trapped. Martin argued that Meacham had made a clean catch of the ball and went off on an expletive-filled tirade at Scott, kicking dirt on the umpire. As a result, Martin was fined $1,000 and suspended for three games.

Without Martin, the Yankees won two out of three in Baltimore and returned home to lose two out of three to the Red Sox.

In Cleveland on June 19, they were routed by the Indians, 11–3, when Martin, obviously intending to prove a point, let pitcher Tim Stoddard absorb a beating that enabled the Indians to build on a 4–3 lead and put the game out of reach. For weeks, Martin had been begging the Yankees to release Stoddard, and his decision to leave Stoddard in to take his lumps was no doubt done to force the issue.

A witness to this was Clyde King, who had been sent by Steinbrenner to observe Martin and report back to the owner. What King reported was that Martin was out of control and the team's pitching was in disarray.

"My advice to you is that we make a change," King told Steinbrenner.

From Cleveland, the Yankees went to Detroit for a three-game series. The Tigers won the first game, 2–1, when reliever Cecilio Guante gave up a home run to Tom Brookens in the 10th inning.

The next night, the Yankees took a 6–1 lead into the bottom of the ninth. The Tigers rallied, and Martin again called on Guante to pitch to Alan Trammell with the bases loaded. Trammell belted a grand slam to climax a six-run rally and give the Tigers a 7–6 victory.

The Tigers won again the next night, scoring a run in the bottom of the 10th for a 3–2 victory in the final game of the series, and the final game of Martin's managerial career.

Steinbrenner had seen enough. He decided to make a change. Martin was fired on June 23 and replaced by Lou Piniella, who just a year before vowed he would never work for Steinbrenner again.

Twenty-two days later, the Yankees released Tim Stoddard. It was vindication, but small consolation, for Billy Martin.

"In all the years I was with Billy," said Judge Eddie Sapir, "I never, ever once saw him in an altercation, and I certainly never saw him initiate one. I've seen crazies come up to him and say, 'You think you're so tough? Well, fight me.'

"When you go back and look at those—let's call them scrapes—that Billy was in, do you wish they had never happened? Absolutely. Billy said he wished they had never happened. But that was his temperament. 'If you start something, I'm not going to walk away.'

"In a couple of them, he didn't have a chance to walk away. The thing with the Marshmallow Man in Minnesota was crazy; two guys making a bet about who could beat who. The truth is what you had there were two willing participants.

"The fight with Ed Whitson? Dale Berra was going to the men's room, and he saw the pitcher being held up in the air by his neck. When Dale told Billy what he saw, and Billy went to assist one of his players, that player turned on Billy.

"The thing in Lace? Billy didn't even know he was in a fight. He didn't know Mickey Mantle had said something to somebody at another table, and the repercussions came back to Billy because Mantle had left the place and the guys he insulted spotted Billy and told the bouncers, 'Yeah, that guy was sitting at the table with him [Mantle].'"

To Sapir and many others who took the time and trouble to know him, Billy Martin was grossly misunderstood, a chameleon, a man of many faces, many moods, and many personalities. He was Dr. Jekyll in street clothes and Mr. Hyde in a baseball uniform. He could be alternately charming and cantankerous, pleasant and pugnacious, cheerful and churlish.

"I don't want to sound like an apologist for Billy because I know he had his faults, and some of the things he did are hard to defend," Sapir said. "But people never understood the other side of Billy Martin.

"One time, around Christmas, Billy and I were on an airplane, and a little boy, who couldn't have been more than eight years old, came over to Billy and asked him for his autograph.

"'Hey, pard,' Billy said, 'where are you going?'

"The kid said he was going to spend Christmas with his mother—it was kind of obvious his parents were divorced.

"'What did you get your mom for Christmas?' Billy asked.

"'Nothing,' the boy said, and with that Billy put his hand in his pocket and took out a $50 bill and handed it to the kid. 'Here,' he said, 'now you buy your momma something nice for Christmas.'

"Billy was always doing something nice for people, for kids, for nuns. He was very generous. One time I got a phone call from some woman who said she had a little boy who was dying of leukemia, and he was a big baseball fan. His mother promised the boy she would take him to the World Series—it was the 1971 Series between Pittsburgh and Baltimore—but she couldn't get tickets.

"I called Billy and asked him if he could do anything. He said, 'How many tickets do you need?' I told him two. He said, 'You got 'em.'

"The next day a package arrived UPS with two tickets for every game.

"There was never a thing for charity that Billy refused to do. If he could do something nice for a good cause, he always wanted to do it.

"That was another common bond between Billy and George Steinbrenner, who is very philanthropic and is always doing things for people, even strangers, that people never hear about. He's sent dozens of kids to college, and he's paid for many funerals of people who died in some tragedy that he read about in the paper, but he never did it for the publicity. I asked George about that once and he said, 'My dad once told me that when you do something nice for somebody and if just you and the person you did it for aren't the only ones who know what you did, then you did it for the wrong reasons.'

"Billy was the same way. When my son was two years old, he had his picture taken with Billy. This was in 1988. I asked Billy to sign the picture, and he wrote, 'To John Paul. God loves you and so do I.' It was signed 'Uncle Billy.'"

EPILOGUE

In the summer of 1989, Billy Martin, out of uniform for a year, was living the life of the gentleman farmer with his fourth wife, Jill Guiver, in Port Crane, New York, just outside Binghamton.

When he left as manager of the Yankees for the fifth time on June 23, 1988, they had a record of 40–28 and were in second place in the American League East. After he left, Martin watched from a distance as the Yankees, under his successor, Lou Piniella, had a record of 45–48, and finished in fifth place.

And Billy Martin waited for a call that never came.

Piniella was fired after the 1988 season and replaced by Dallas Green, who would last five months on the job.

And Billy Martin waited for a call that never came.

Sure, he had been "fired" as manager of the Yankees five times by George Steinbrenner; but he had been hired to manage the Yankees by Steinbrenner five times, and he believed in his heart that a Billy VI was soon to happen. He had, in fact, begun making plans to manage the Yankees again in 1990. He had contacted a few of his closest associates and alerted them to be ready to go to work as coaches for him.

That was Martin's mindset that summer when I visited him on his farm. As president of the Baseball Writers' Association of America, it was my duty to take part in the annual Hall of Fame induction ceremonies in Cooperstown, and I availed myself of the opportunity to plan a vacation trip with my 14-year-old son, John. After Cooperstown, we would make a tour of minor league baseball in upstate New York, seven games in eight days.

I had called Martin in advance to tell him about my plans and asked him if he would be receptive to a visit from my son and me. He said we would be more than welcome. In fact, he seemed eager about it.

We arrived at the Martin farm shortly after noon. Billy had thoughtfully arranged for a local college student to keep my son occupied and entertained by taking him fishing on a lake on Martin's property while he and I talked.

Martin looked rested and relaxed, healthier than I had seen him in years, and he seemed content in the role of country squire. I found him in a rare nostalgic and contemplative mood, reflecting on his past and coming to grips, if somewhat regretfully, with his own idiosyncrasies.

"Sometimes I think my reputation has preceded me to the point that people prejudge me," he said. "I'll meet somebody for the first time, and the guy will go to shake my hand, and he'll hold out his hand tentatively. 'Don't hit me now,' he'll say. That bothers me. It's like I'm Ty Cobb, who spiked everybody who got in his way. It bothers me because that's not the real Billy Martin.

"There are two Billy Martins. There's one Billy Martin when I'm at the ballpark and a second Billy Martin when I'm away from the ballpark. It's like a mask comes over my face once I get to the ballpark. I don't know why it happens, but it happens. I'll drive to the stadium and park my car, and as soon as I get out of the car and walk into the stadium, I become another person. It's not intentional. I don't know why or how, it just happens.

"I'm not someone who has ever been a perfectionist when it comes to neatness and order. In fact, I'm a bit of a slob at times. Now, all of a sudden, at the ballpark, as a manager, I become a perfectionist. There's nothing else in my life that I have ever worked as hard at as my job on the baseball field.

"A lot of people don't understand me. I'm a man first, and then I'm a manager. I'm a human being. I'm a father. I'm a grandfather. I'm a son. I'm a brother. And I'm a Christian. I go to church. I always have. I don't flaunt my faith. I don't wear it on my sleeve, but I always wear a tiny gold cross in my baseball cap as an expression of my faith. I'm not a perfect human being. My language isn't always the greatest, and I lose my temper more than I should. I'm not trying to justify my behavior or ask anyone to condone it, but I want people to know that I try to live the life of a good Christian."

I learned something else about Billy Martin that day. He is a gracious host and a good cook. When we arrived, he asked my son if he liked spaghetti, and John said he did. As we talked, Billy busied himself preparing a spaghetti dinner for my son and me.

At the time, Martin was still on the Yankee payroll and employed by WPIX-TV as an occasional analyst on Yankee games. I asked him if he was content.

"I'm enjoying life," he said, "but deep down, I believe I'm wasting my talent. The thing I do best is not talking on television. The thing I do best is manage a baseball team."

"My father loved everything about baseball," said Billy Martin Jr. "He felt he knew the game. He was also smart enough to know that nobody knows everything about this game. The game lived in him. It meant so much to him. He was not a big fan of superstars. He always felt he could win with a group of guys that maybe had a little bit less talent, but would run through a wall for him."

After dinner, Billy Martin and I said our good-byes, and my son and I headed home. It would be the last time I saw Billy.

A few weeks later, on August 18, with the Yankees stuck in sixth place with a record of 56–65, seven and a half games out of first, Dallas Green was fired.

And Billy Martin waited for a call that did not come.

To replace Green, Steinbrenner chose Bucky Dent, who had been managing the Bombers' AAA farm team at Columbus in the International League.

"Billy had a problem," Steinbrenner said. "I used to tell him, 'Billy, you'll be killed by this problem. It won't be any other way. This problem will end up getting you if you don't stop it.'

"That was the drinking and getting into fights all the time. I just couldn't get him to stop. He remained a dear friend of mine. He was a brilliant, brilliant manager. He was a hip pocket manager. He carried it all in his hip pocket and in his head. But it was constantly this problem that he had. I remember sitting with him at dinner and talking to him, trying to make him understand.

"'Billy, this thing is going to kill you if you don't stop it,' I said. 'You've got to stop it.' He'd nod his head, but in the end, that's what got him."

If Billy Martin were alive today, he surely would be amused by the preoccupation with his (legal) alcohol consumption, while all around him (illegally) chemically enhanced athletes with bloated heads and physiques are smashing long-revered records.

On Christmas Day, 1989, Bill Reedy, Martin's friend from Detroit, visited Martin's home. While Billy's wife, Jill, prepared Christmas dinner, Martin and Reedy decided to drive to a local pub for some holiday cheer.

They had a few drinks—maybe more than a few—and headed back home on icy roads. Martin's SUV hit a patch of ice and slammed into a culvert leading to his property.

At 5:45 p.m., in Wilson Memorial Hospital in nearby Johnson City, Billy Martin was pronounced dead, still waiting for the phone call that never came.

On May 15, 2007, 19 years after he managed his last game, 18 years after his death, Billy Martin's legacy lived on in a game at Shea Stadium between the Mets, managed by Willie Randolph, and the Cubs, managed by Lou Piniella, two of Billy's Boys. Randolph had played for him. Piniella had played for him, coached under him, and succeeded him as manager of the Yankees. Martin was their mentor, their teacher, their role model.

If Billy were alive today, "he would absolutely hate all this fraternization that goes on in baseball," Randolph told Bill Madden of the *New York Daily News*. "Billy believed in an us against the world mentality, and we fed off that. Everyone hated the Yankees, everyone wanted to beat the Yankees. We talked about that, and Billy liked that attitude that we brought to the table every day, where we were fighting everyone.

"We didn't fraternize, and if you did, he fined you. As a young player, I thought that was really very cool. We developed a swagger under him, a little bit of a chip on the shoulder."

"I remember you never saw Billy talking to opposing players," Piniella said. "And if we did, he'd tell us, 'Say hello and that's it.'"

"Watching Lou and the way he manages," said Randolph, "he reminds me so much of Billy in that he's always in the game and trying to have an impact. You know he's going to employ all the little things that can beat you. You have to expect the unexpected."

The legacy of Billy Martin is in the people who played for him and coached for him and went on to become managers themselves, taking a part of Billy with them. It's in Piniella and Randolph, in Charlie Manuel, Frank Quilici, Gene Lamont, and Frank Howard. It's in Jim Fregosi, Mike Hargrove, Dick Howser, and Bob Lemon. It's in Bucky Dent, Don Baylor, Jackie Moore, and Davey Lopes; all of them Billy's Boys; all of them touched, in some way, by Martin.

Had he lived, would there have been a Billy VI with the Yankees?

We'll never know.

Martin went to his death with the thought that he would return for another stint as manager of the Yankees, maybe the following season, and his friend and lawyer, Judge Eddie Sapir of New Orleans, believed a Billy VI was inevitable.

But that may have been wishful thinking on Martin's part. It was not going to happen, as Martin hoped, with the start of spring training, 1990. Bucky Dent had been hired the previous August, and he would be the Yankees manager in 1990.

It might have happened when Dent was fired on June 6, 1990, and replaced by Stump Merrill had Martin not died five months before.

George Steinbrenner, however, said a Billy VI was not in the offing.

"No way," Steinbrenner told the *New York Times* the day after Martin's death. "He was too happy doing what he was doing. He was coming upstairs. He was going to be there more than ever before. He was enthused about the coming season. In the past, it was a hit and miss thing, but he was going to be working a lot. I must have talked to him 20 times in the last month and a half."

"When I first hired him, his mother called me and asked for an autographed picture, and I sent it. He told me that 'every time you'd fire me, my mother put the picture in the john. When you hired me, she put it above her dresser.'"

If he were alive today, would Billy Martin be the swashbuckling, fiery, feisty manager with the rare ability to provide the quick fix, to make instant winners out of chronic losers?

It's doubtful because the game has changed, players have changed, managing has changed, and Martin never could change.

It is difficult contemplating Martin managing today, with pitch counts, radar guns, and computers, with players who don't bust it all the time, every time, and with the proliferation of the media and its constant, endless scrutiny.

"I don't know if Billy could manage today," said Rod Carew. "All he asked of you as a manager was when you get between the lines, you give it your all, and if you did, he would never say anything to embarrass you. Just play hard, that's all he asked you to do. After the game, you could run, you could do whatever you want, but just give it a full effort in the game. That's all he asked of any of his players."

As a manager, Martin was old school. Where he came from, pitchers pitched complete games, they finished what they started, they stayed in games as long as they were effective without regard to the number of pitches they threw.

Computer printouts? Martin never believed in them. He managed on instinct, made decisions from the seat of his pants, from his gut, and from his head. He never needed a printout to tell him how this hitter fared against that pitcher, or how this pitcher fared against that hitter.

"The problem with computers," Martin once said, "is that they are only as good as the brain that programs them and feeds them. If you have a dummy putting the data in the computer, what good is the computer?

"There are some things a computer can't tell you. It can't tell you the situation in the game when an individual got a hit off a certain pitcher. It doesn't tell you what the score was at the time, what inning it was, what the count was on the hitter. A computer doesn't measure aggressiveness, hustle, and the heart of a player. All it tells you is plain, cold statistics, and statistics don't tell the whole story. I'd much rather trust my eyes, or the eyes of one of my scouts, than a computer."

Martin often was curt, caustic, crude, and combative with the media. He had come from a time when writers covering baseball teams rarely visited the clubhouse after games to talk with players or managers. They functioned like theater critics, writing their stories from the press box, reporting, analyzing, critiquing, pontificating, their stories rarely, almost never, containing quotes.

Martin preferred it that way, and came to expect that, and the practice continued in his early days as a manager in places like Minnesota, Detroit, and Texas where the press corps assigned to cover his team might be made up of two or three reporters.

New York was different. There the press corps was a horde swarming around the Yankees.

Martin, most times, was unapproachable and uncooperative. He was, at all times, never gracious in defeat. How could he be when he took losing so hard? He found it painful to sit in his office, at his desk, and have to explain why he had failed that day, and so he often ducked the issue by retreating to the players' lounge (off-limits to the media) or the trainers' room (also off-limits to the media) and making himself unavailable.

In dealing with the media, again, there were two Billy Martins. A reporter had to earn his or her stripes with Martin, earn his trust and his confidence, in order to enter his inner circle. With those who regularly covered his team, those who knew him as a player or as a manager with other teams, he could be helpful, forthcoming, and informative.

But he had little patience with young reporters he did not know, or those who showed up at the ballpark sporadically.

As one who was able to enter Martin's inner circle, I would often listen to how he dealt with some members of the media, and I would cringe inwardly, thinking, "Billy, why must you be so contentious? "Why can't you be charming and gracious as I know you can be? If you were, you could have these people eating out of your hand."

In his own defense, Martin admitted, "I'm sometimes a little too rough on some young writers. I don't mean to be, but I don't have any time or patience for stupid questions. I prepare for every game. I do my homework, so why can't these writers prepare as I do? Why can't they do their homework like I do? I may be rough on them, or short-tempered with them, and I know that creates a bad image, and I know I'll never be able to change that image."

As owner and as manager of the New York Yankees, George Steinbrenner and Billy Martin made beautiful music in their two first full seasons together with two American League pennants and one World Series championship . . . and a lot of noise, a cacophony that reverberated across the baseball landscape and still resonates to this day.

Theirs was a match made in heaven, but it couldn't last and it couldn't be repeated, and that union lit fires that raged out of control for 14 years.

With five marriages and five divorces, they were baseball's equivalent of Richard Burton and Elizabeth Taylor, who married twice in the 1960s and 1970s. Like Burton and Taylor, Steinbrenner and Martin apparently couldn't live together, and they couldn't live apart.

Said Judge Eddie Sapir: "It was crystal clear to me that George really liked Billy and wanted to have him around, and being a Yankee in some capacity was something that Billy Martin genuinely wanted to do. I will concede that he preferred managing, but that was something that was out of his control. A couple of times, unfortunately, we had some incidents along the way, and perhaps that prompted George to make a decision to put Billy in another position.

"If George made a decision one day that Billy wouldn't be his manager, we all know they could have said good-bye, and George never wanted to do that. He wanted to structure something that was acceptable to Billy in case George ever wanted to make that change. What we came up with was very acceptable to Billy.

"At first we structured a contract that had Billy performing several jobs for the Yankees. If George would opt for Billy not to manage anymore and to step into some other position, then two things would happen: One, Billy would get a bonus, and two, his contract would be extended.

"We did this several times until George said, 'You know what, Eddie? I'd really like to take care of Billy for his life. Why don't we do something for Billy for a lifetime, even when he can no longer come to spring training, when it won't make any difference whether he performs a service for the Yankees or not, because this is a good guy, and I don't want him to be penniless or be in a situation where he doesn't have any money coming in.'

"I said, 'I think that's wonderful, George, and very generous of you.' We were both looking down the road at an elderly Billy, needing a handsome check from the New York Yankees each year even when he couldn't provide a service. This way we knew that Billy always would have—it was either $200,000 or $300,000, I forget the exact amount—coming in every year of his life."

If he were alive today, Martin would have a hard time understanding how George Steinbrenner, who hired him five times and fired him five times, who changed managers 17 times in 17 years, found the patience to live with the same manager, Joe Torre, for 12 seasons. And it surely would have made him envious.

"I would like to work for an owner who really appreciated what I do out there," Martin once said. "I would like to work for somebody who appreciates that I put my heart into it when I manage and who realizes I know what I'm doing and let's me run the show without any interference."

Billy Martin never had an owner like that. Maybe, he had only himself to blame.

Appendix: Timeline of Key Events

January 3, 1973—George M. Steinbrenner III of Lorain, Ohio, heads up a limited partnership that purchases the Yankees from the Columbia Broadcasting System for $10 million, some $3 million less than CBS paid for the team eight years earlier.

September 30, 1973—Ralph Houk resigns as manager of the Yankees, with whom he had been associated for almost three decades as a player, minor league manager, coach, major league manager, and general manager.

January 3, 1974—Bill Virdon is named manager of the Yankees after attempts to hire Dick Williams away from the Oakland Athletics are thwarted.

April 5, 1974—George M. Steinbrenner III is indicted by a federal grand jury on 14 felony counts in connection with illegal campaign contributions to Richard Nixon's Committee to Re-elect the President by Steinbrenner's American Shipbuilding Company. On the day before the start of the major league baseball season, Steinbrenner voluntarily removes himself from the daily affairs of the Yankees pending further investigation of the charges.

Appendix

November 27, 1974—George Steinbrenner begins a two-year suspension from baseball imposed by Commissioner Bowie Kuhn.

December 31, 1974—The Yankees sign pitcher Jim "Catfish" Hunter as a free agent to a record five-year, $3.75 million contract.

July 21, 1975—Billy Martin is fired as manager of the Texas Rangers.

August 2, 1975—Billy Martin replaces Bill Virdon as manager of the Yankees. "It's the only job I ever wanted," Martin says.

April 15, 1976—After spending two seasons in their temporary home, Shea Stadium, the Yankees return to a remodeled Yankee Stadium.

October 14, 1976—Chris Chambliss's leadoff home run in the bottom of the ninth in Game 5 of the American League Championship Series against the Kansas City Royals gives the Yankees their 30th American League pennant and their first in 12 years.

October 21, 1976—The Cincinnati Reds complete a four-game sweep of the Yankees in the World Series. After the final game, George Steinbrenner storms into the Yankee clubhouse, accosts a sobbing Billy Martin, and issues a not-so-veiled threat. "We won a pennant," Steinbrenner rages, "but I want a [World Series] ring."

November 29, 1976—Reggie Jackson signs a five-year, $2.96 million free agent contract with the Yankees.

March 26, 1977—After losing an exhibition game to the Yankees' crosstown rivals, the Mets, George Steinbrenner takes out his frustration on Billy Martin. Already angry because his manager has refused to ride on the team bus, choosing instead to drive his own car to and from games, Steinbrenner threatens to fire Martin. Martin responds by slamming his fist against an ice bucket, splattering cubes onto Steinbrenner and team president Gabe Paul.

March 27, 1977—Gabe Paul brings George Steinbrenner and Billy Martin together over breakfast and brokers a truce between the two men.

May 9, 1977—George Steinbrenner fines Billy Martin $2,500 for insubordination after Martin complains to the press that Steinbrenner has ignored his request to bring veteran catcher Elrod Hendricks up from the minor leagues.

May 19, 1977—Controversy explodes on the Yankees with publication of a *Sport* magazine article in which Reggie Jackson is quoted as saying, "I'm the straw that stirs the drink. . . . [Thurman] Munson thinks he can stir the drink, but he can only stir it bad." The article splits the Yankees into two factions, those who are pro-Munson and those (few) who are pro-Jackson. Stung by the remarks, Munson refuses to shake Jackson's hand after Reggie hits a home run.

June 18, 1977—Billy Martin removes Reggie Jackson from right field in Boston's Fenway Park, accusing him of failing to hustle on a double by Jim Rice of the Red Sox. Martin and Jackson almost come to blows in the dugout and have to be separated by coaches Yogi Berra and Elston Howard. Watching the ugly scene on television, George Steinbrenner is irate. Once more he threatens to fire his manager.

June 19, 1977—Once again Gabe Paul acts as peacemaker. He intervenes with Steinbrenner to save Martin's job and brings Martin and Jackson together. They reach an accord, and Steinbrenner backs off his threat to fire his manager. Steinbrenner issues a list of seven commandments by which a manager should be judged.

August 10, 1977—Billy Martin relents and installs Reggie Jackson in the No. 4 batting position. Jackson responds by hitting 13 home runs and driving in 49 runs in the final 53 games of the season.

October 9, 1977—Billy Martin puts his job on the line by benching Reggie Jackson in Game 5 of the American League Championship Series against the Kansas City Royals. Trailing 3–1 in the eighth inning, Martin calls on Jackson as a pinch hitter, and Reggie comes through with an RBI single to make it 3–2. The Yankees score three runs in the ninth for a 5–3 victory and their second straight American League pennant under Martin.

October 16, 1977—Reggie Jackson hits three home runs on three consecutive pitches in Game 6 of the World Series against the Los Angeles Dodgers. The Yankees win the game, and the Series, their first in 15 years.

July 17, 1978—Billy Martin gives Reggie Jackson the bunt sign in the 10th inning of a 5–5 tie with the Kansas City Royals. Insulted by being asked to bunt, Jackson makes a halfhearted attempt to bunt. Martin removes the bunt sign and gives Jackson the hit sign. Defiantly, Reggie bunts anyway and pops out. Martin is livid. He suspends Jackson, a decision supported by George Steinbrenner.

July 24, 1978—One day after telling to reporters, "They [Reggie Jackson and George Steinbrenner] deserve each other: One's a born liar, the other's convicted," Billy Martin tearfully "resigns" as manager of the Yankees. He is replaced by Bob Lemon.

July 29, 1978—In a shocking turn of events, the Yankees announce that Billy Martin will return to manage the team in 1980, with Bob Lemon moving up to general manager.

November 10, 1978—Billy Martin brawls with Reno sportswriter Ray Hagar.

June 18, 1979—Billy Martin returns as manager of the Yankees, replacing Bob Lemon nine months before planned.

August 2, 1979—Yankees catcher and captain Thurman Munson is killed at the age of 32 when his private plane crashes in Canton, Ohio.

October 23, 1979—Billy Martin punches out Joseph Cooper, a 52-year-old marshmallow salesman, in a Minnesota hotel bar.

October 28, 1979—The Yankees announce that Billy Martin has been relieved of his duties as manager of the Yankees and replaced by third base coach Dick Howser.

October 10, 1981—After leading the Oakland Athletics to the American League West division championship with a brand of exciting baseball called "BillyBall," the A's, under manager Billy Martin, are swept by the Yankees in a three-game American League Championship Series.

October 20, 1982—The Oakland Athletics fire Billy Martin as manager.

January 11, 1983—Eighty-four days after the Oakland Athletics fired him, Billy Martin is hired to manage the Yankees for the third time.

December 16, 1983—Billy Martin is fired as manager of the Yankees for the third time.

April 28, 1985—Yogi Berra, who George Steinbrenner said would be his manager for the entire season, "no matter what," is fired after 16 games. His successor will be Billy Martin, returning to manage the Yankees for the fourth time.

September 20, 1985—Billy Martin engages in a fight with pitcher Ed Whitson in a Baltimore hotel bar. Martin arrives at the ballpark the following day with a cast on his broken right arm.

October 27, 1985—Billy IV ends when Martin is fired as manager of the Yankees and replaced by Lou Piniella.

August 10, 1986—George Steinbrenner fulfills a promise by staging Billy Martin Day at Yankee Stadium. Martin's uniform No. 1 is retired.

October 19, 1987—The Yankees announce that Lou Piniella will not return as manager in 1988. Billy Martin, who will take the job for the fifth time, will replace him.

May 6, 1988—Billy Martin is beaten into a bloody pulp by bouncers at Lace, an Arlington, Texas, topless club.

June 23, 1988—Billy Martin is fired as manager of the Yankees for the fifth time, and, for the second time, he is replaced by Lou Piniella.

December 25, 1989—Billy Martin is killed at the age of 61 when his car hits a culvert at the entrance to his home in Port Crane, New York. At the time Martin believed he was going to return to manage the Yankees for a sixth tour.

November 1, 2007—After reigning for 35 seasons, King George Steinbrenner is taking steps to abdicate his throne by turning over control of the Yankees to his sons, Hank and Hal. Steinbrenner, who turned 77 on July 4, no longer is the visible, blustery, involved owner of the past. He is rarely seen in public and heard even more infrequently, choosing to communicate through statements released by his public relations representative.

In 2007, their penultimate season in Yankee Stadium (a new Yankee Stadium will open in the 2009 season), the Yankees drew 4,271,867 fans, the second-largest total in baseball history and their third straight year over four million.

Under Steinbrenner's watch, the Yankees have increased in value from $10 million to an estimated $1.5 billion. In addition, the YES (Yankees Entertainment & Sports) Network is said to be valued in excess of $3 billion.

Bibliography

Allen, Maury. *Damn Yankee*. New York: Times Books, 1980.

Ford, Whitey, with Phil Pepe. *Slick: My Life in and around Baseball*. New York: William Morrow, 1987.

Golenbock, Peter. *Wild, High and Tight: The Life and Death of Billy Martin*. New York: St. Martin's Press, 1994.

Jackson, Reggie, with Mike Lupica. *Reggie*. New York: Villard, 1984.

Kuhn, Bowie. *Hardball*. New York: Times Books, 1987.

Lyle, Sparky, and Peter Golenbock. *The Bronx Zoo*. New York: Crown, 1979.

Madden, Bill, and Moss Klein. *Damned Yankees: A No-Holds-Barred Account of Life with "Boss" Steinbrenner*. New York: Warner Books, 1990.

Mahler, Jonathan. *The Bronx Is Burning*. New York: Farrar, Straus and Giroux, 2005.

Mantle, Mickey, and Phil Pepe. *My Favorite Summer 1956*. New York: Doubleday, 1991.

Martin, Billy, and Peter Golenbock. *Number 1*. New York: Delacorte Press, 1980.

Martin, Billy, with Phil Pepe. *BillyBall*. New York: Doubleday, 1987.

Bibliography

Nettles, Graig, and Peter Golenbock. *Balls*. New York: Putnam, 1984.

Pepe, Phil. *Talkin' Baseball: An Oral History of Baseball in the 1970s*. New York: Random House, 1998.

Schaap, Dick. *Steinbrenner*. New York: Putnam, 1982.

Smith, Norman Lewis. *The Return of Billy the Kid*. New York: Coward, McCann & Geoghegan, 1977.

Index

Index

Index

Index

Index

Index

About the Author

Phil Pepe has covered sports in New York for more than five decades. He was the Yankees beat writer for the *New York World Telegram & Sun* from 1961–1964, and for the *New York Daily News* from 1971–1984. He is the author of more than 40 books, including *My Favorite Summer 1956* with Mickey Mantle, *BillyBall* with Billy Martin, and *Talkin' Baseball: An Oral History of Baseball in the 1970s*. He lives in Englewood, New Jersey.

COURTESY BASEBALL WRITERS ASSOCIATION
OF AMERICA, NEW YORK CHAPTER